FIFTY YEARS
A PLANEMAKER
AND USER

Cecil E. Pierce

Southport, Maine

With drawings by Sam Manning

The Monmouth Press

Monmouth, Maine

ISBN 0-9628001-1-2
Library of Congress Catalog Card Number
92-60195

Published by the Monmouth Press
Monmouth, Maine
Manufactured in the United States of America
First Printing

In Memory

I dedicate this book to Lucy,
a wife who tolerated my considerable idiosyncracies
throughout this long life.

A Page of Gratitude

To Barbara Rumsey: She transformed my incomplete sentences and incorrect punctuation into readable prose.

To Sam Manning and his wife Susan: He gave me the unfailingly accurate drawings for which he is justly famous. They gave me encouragement, advice and hospitality.

To Beverly Phifer: She deciphered my longhand, which is near hieroglyphic, and with the aid of her computer reproduced it in typescript.

To friend and craftsman Maurice Sherman, who never lost the faith and who did the amateur photography.

To the Monmouth Press: The people there took my chaotic and rough material and polished it into this format.

Without them this book would have been impossible.

Contents

Preface

This romance with the plane is not the story of one who has earned his cornflakes and milk solely from the making and using of wooden planes, but rather the story of one whose long life has been, to a large degree, the working of wood.

This is the diversification of endeavors from machine shop to boat building and home building, with planemaking sandwiched in between. There has always been in the background of my mind, in my dreams, and underway on my bench, a new plane: one to exceed all others either in workmanship or the use of an even more exotic wood, or, what is most unlikely at this late date, a breakthrough in design. I believe that I have accomplished the latter.

I pen this book that I may somehow inspire even a few to make certain that this art is not lost to time. If I succeed in this my reward will be immense.

If I were to offer advice to this "few," no matter how diverse and unknown they may be, my words would be short and sweet: "Never be satisfied."

That has been, and still is, my creed.

Cecil E. Pierce
Planemaker

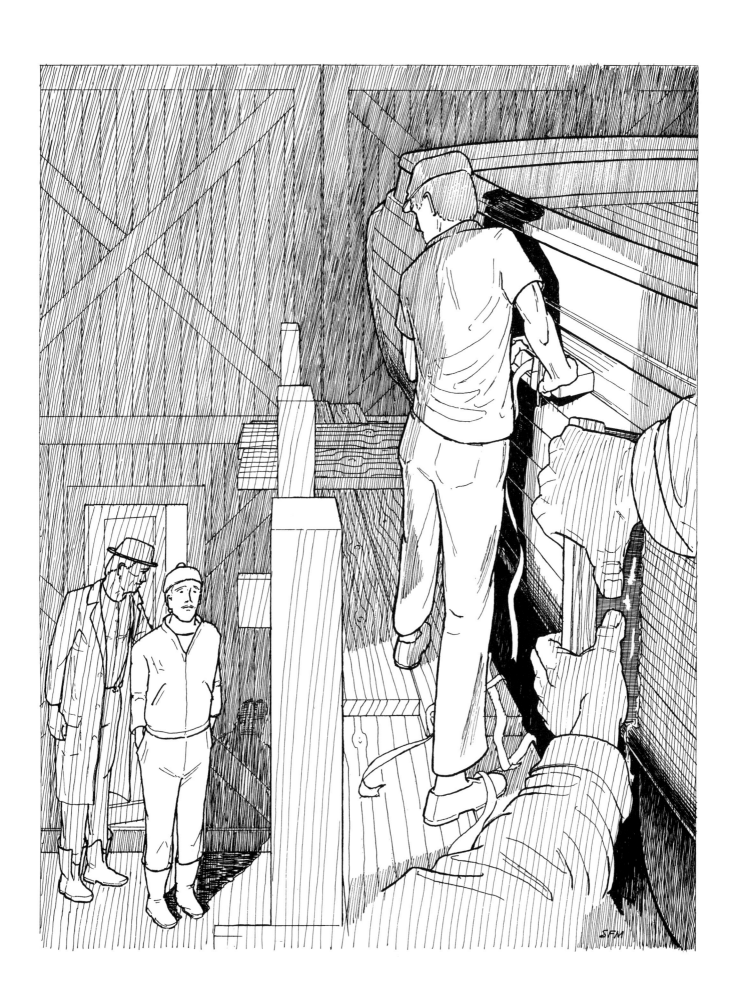

Introduction

It was about sixty-five years ago that I had a chance meeting with my uncle somewhere in town, probably at the local general store.

"Cecil," he said, "let's you and me go to East Boothbay and visit the shipyards tomorrow."

Uncle was not fooling me about his intentions; his motive was not to show me around but to get there himself. He had no auto and he knew that I had an old Model T that would take us the fifteen miles very well, even though it was spring and the roads were muddy and riddled with frost and ruts.

Like the ship that sailed with the tide in the morning, we set out and we arrived in due time without incident. Uncle Fred opened the little door in the big door and stepped inside with me close at his heels. There before our eyes was a schooner yacht newly planked up. High on a staging on her side were two men.

These were the days of the entrepreneurial outboard jointers. One was taking long sweeps with a wooden plane and was sending to the floor shavings as long and unbroken as his step-back and lunge-ahead allowed.

Close behind him was another man with a turned-edge scraper doing the same thing, only the shavings were so thin that they defied gravity to bring them down. Feathers would have wafted down more quickly.

After a few minutes of watching this show, my uncle, himself a veteran of boatyard work, called out to the man with the scraper, "God, don't I wish that I could sharpen a scraper like that."

My young and fertile mind was to become pregnant with that scene and my uncle's words of incredulity. I cannot tell you of anything else that I saw that day, although we visited two other yards; nothing else mattered.

Although the period of gestation was to be a long one, I was determined to master the plane and the scraper. Thus, that chance meeting was to influence me for the rest of my life. So here I will attempt to pass on to you all that I have learned on the subject.

The Exotic Plane Woods

To me, selecting the wood for the next plane is one of the great joys. I caress it as if it had a heart and soul rather than being an inanimate object. If it is a species new to me, working some of the scrap pieces will alert me to any of the hidden idiosyncracies of its anatomy. Then, taking the first step by squaring it up lovingly under the smooth plane and turned-edge scraper.

Following are some – not all – of the woods that I have worked into planes, and my assessment of them.

LIGNUM VITAE is as wonderful as some of the following woods are for our purpose. This wood, with its specific gravity of 1.23 plus its near frictionless surface, has to be rated as pre-eminent among them all. I have never seen a plane of this wood that was worn out or beyond restoration with minor work.

A few years ago at a yard sale, I bought for fifteen dollars a horribly abused lignum vitae razeed jack plane. My reason for buying it was the fine, little used, Charles Buck cast steel "iron" that was in it – doubtless a replacement. With no intention of doing anything but adding the iron to my inventory of irons and discarding the body, I took it home.

I did as I planned with the iron, but my respect for the wood would not allow me to throw it away. I cut an inch and a half off the beat-up tail end, glued on a large piece of the same wood to a bottom front corner, and replaced the missing handle.

Next, I fitted an Ohio Tool Co. cast steel iron which I had mistakenly judged not worthy of a new plane. That Ohio is as good as any tool that I own in its ability to take a keen edge and hold it. This old restored tool gets used as much as any in the shop. I use two more smaller planes of this wood with a similar story.

This wood works with a reasonable ease. No matter how long it is dried, some minor cracks will develop when you open it up. The color ranges from near black to light brown with white sapwood edges. This latter makes a beautiful plane.

VERA WOOD. I have made two planes of this handsome, greenish, interlocked-grain, heavy wood. It works quite similarly to the above lignum. I do not know any more about it than that. I would use it again if I could get it.

Coco Bolo. Beautiful, traditional, obtainable, and expensive. I have used it many times and expect to again. This is one of the world's several rosewoods. They all fight you back when you work them. They smell like roses when they are heated by the action of power tools or even hand tools, hence the name.

Some other rosewood species that I have used for planes are: East Indian, Mexican, Brazilian, Purple Heart, and Brazilian Tulipwood. All have a specific gravity of .85 or higher.

Macassar Ebony. Ah! Here is a plane wood par excellence! Beautiful deep dark brown, near black, with off-white streaks. It is as hard as the proverbial prostitute's heart. Your tools and mettle will get tested working this wood.

I once made three planes from the same plank of this ebony: a short smoother, a jack, and a short joiner. All had matching Moulson Bros. irons and crotch red oak handles. Such satisfaction comes but seldom in a lifetime.

These trees grow in the Macassar Straits area of the Indian Ocean. Musical instrument makers are partial to this wood and term it Indian ebony. The specific gravity is up there at 1.09. I love this wood.

Black Mango. This is another wood about which I know little. I came by a piece of it through a friend and neighbor who spends his winters in Florida. When he returned a few springs ago, he had for me a piece of wood which was very heavy and near black. He said it was black mango. He had gotten it from a neighbor's firewood pile down there. When he told the neighbor he would like to take it north to a planemaker, the reply was, "It won't be any use to him. It is too hard to be worked." Well, that man was very nearly right.

It was a round stick and not very dry. I took off four small slabs with the bandsaw and put it away. But not for very long. It beckoned me to work it – rather too soon. Anyway, I worked it into a plane.

In a year or so it had warped its bottom so that it had to be resurfaced. But, for all of this drying-out and working, there was not a crack came anywhere in it. It could not crack because God had laid up its growth rings like plywood.

I use and enjoy this plane, with its I. & H. Sorby iron, on my bench nearly every day. I wonder if anyone else has ever used this very suitable wood for a plane. I would like to have some more of it.

Some suitable and relatively cheap native woods of my experience follow:

ROCK MAPLE: easily obtainable. It grows in the northeast U.S.A., especially my native Maine.

BEECH: the favored wood of the volume planemakers of another era. It is plentiful and easily worked. The European species is even more easily worked and just as popular with the European planemakers.

PECAN: a beautiful wood, at least my piece was, with its dark brown, sparsely located patches of color. It is of the hickory family.

I found it to be coarse-grained; therefore, it should not be rated highly as a plane wood.

MESQUITE (HONEY LOCUST, IRONWOOD): grows in the southwest U.S.A. Just the name alone engendered respect in the joiner shops of the northeast yacht-building yards. With its rather high specific gravity of .80, I recommend mesquite.

APPLE WOOD: here is a wood that with little effort one can get free. It needs a long drying period, as it warps considerably in the process. The apple wood of the northeast has woodpecker blemishes throughout its wood. I think this enhances it, though others may disagree.

Here is what happens. In its growing years, the bark is completely peppered by woodpeckers, their holes reaching through to the cambium layer. This causes the tree to bleed its sweetish sap, attracting winged insects. The woodpecker is not interested in the sap. The insects are its quarry and sustenance.

This wood, in spite of its specific gravity of .71, will make an excellent plane. In addition, it is an excellent and traditional tool-handle wood. I keep lots of it under the bench.

This list could go on ad infinitum. So I will close this section with the last-named wood. My one regret is that I cannot list and report on snakewood, perhaps the heaviest of them, with its specific gravity of 1.30. It is on my "most wanted" list.

The Irons

CAST STEEL: One hundred and twenty-five toolmakers in England and the U.S.A. made woodworking tools of the stuff. They proudly stamped their name and logo on their products, along with the words "cast steel" – usually prefixed with "warranted." This is the finest steel ever produced to take and hold a keen edge for the working of wood by hand tools.

What is this near-magical wording, "cast steel"? Isn't all steel cast at some time? Yes, it is. I have searched for the answer but it eludes me.

After wading through two large books on steelmaking, it seems to me that the essence of the process goes thus.

First, it has to be puddled while melting in the furnace. This is done by two men with long rods reaching in and working the impurities to the top and to one side, rather like a chef stirring his stew. This, of course, demands that the "melts" be small.

The labor-intensiveness and the small batch are enough to doom it in today's business atmosphere of high production. It is no longer made.

Be that as it may, the fact is that the steel companies had a very superior product to sell to the toolmakers. It was so comparatively costly that the toolmakers used only a small piece of it and hammer-welded it to a piece of wrought iron. Then, the whole was shaped into the familiar "iron."

Why wrought iron instead of mild steel? I know not. Perhaps wrought iron made a better weld under the hammer. It is more probable that it was cheaper than mild steel and served the purpose as well.

I have made irons from tungsten carbide, high-speed steel – these two will turn red-hot chips from steel in a lathe – carbon steel, even mushet.

Mushet, what's that?

It certainly dates me, does it not?

These were all found wanting for hand tools. No one makes cast steel any more and I won't use anything else. Where do I get it? Yard sales and antique tool dealers.

I have a large inventory of these choice irons, which I have bought from the above sources. The gem of them all, and perhaps of my entire tool collection, is an unopened package of six irons made and tied up perhaps a hundred years ago by Isaac Greaves of Sheffield.

Just imagine, no one has seen these irons since that long-ago workman wrapped them up in their heavy paper and pasted on a blue and gold label of "C" and "S": scrolls proclaiming them "warranted of superior quality," then a second plain label reading "warranted cast steel." He then tied it all up securely with three turns of flax cord.

I never in my lifetime will undo his work. Come to the inevitable auction when this is all over. You can probably nearly steal them from some unknowledgeable auctioneer.

Upon more sober reflection, when I can no longer protect them, some "heartless wretch" will have torn them open. The secret will be out. I bought three packages of these irons and opened one of them, so I know of their superior quality. I put them in two adjustable throat smooth planes.

Were these "irons" from a hundred different makers consistent in their quality? Back in the years when I practically worshipped a Wm. Ash, and I. & H. Sorby, or a Charles Buck, I thought them a mile ahead; oh well, a half mile anyway. But now I see no pariahs, only kings. Any difference would have to have been in the tempering, as all of them were likely to have used the same, or very similar, raw steel from the mill.

Those men who did the tempering were, of course, skilled at their job of dunking at just the right moment, the moment being determined by the color change of the cooling steel.

A good example of this was brought home to me one day as I walked down through the boatyard with the late Arthur Stevens. As we walked by a man at work with an adze, Arthur stopped and said, "How's it going, John?"

"Everything would be all right if I could get my adze tempered right. Soft!"

What he left unsaid was well understood by us. From much sharpening, his adze had worn back to where it was too thick to sharpen well. So, he had taken it to the blacksmith to be "drawn out." This meant heating and hammering on the anvil to the desired thinness. This, of course, entailed the losing of its temper. In retempering it, the old blacksmith, being afraid of getting it too hard, had erred to the soft side. Too hard and the tool would break and that would be ruinous to both the tool and the blacksmith's reputation.

Planes Down the Ages

"To 500 feet clearboards for OGs"
Gershom Flagg invoice for building
Pownalborough, Maine Courthouse, 1760

It is not my intention or the purpose of this book to get deeply into the history of the plane. Such has been well covered by others more qualified to do so than me.

The genesis goes something like this. Way back in the dim history of man and the discovery of iron some smith, by accident and good fortune, discovered that the constant heating and hammering of the new metal made it harder, and by quenching it in water, it became harder yet. He did not know why this was so.

Today, we know that the constant and multiple heating of the iron caused it to absorb carbon from the coal fire. This carbon is a necessary ingredient of tool steel.

The attendant hammering also refined the grain of the iron, which was another plus.

The result of this process was tool steel, without which we cannot have a plane.

The rest is easy: a piece of this new wonderful material is quickly set in a suitable piece of wood and wedged in place – the basic ingredients of a hand plane. Man has continually improved them to this day. It is the third most necessary tool after the hammer and the saw.

The wooden plane was to remain the only plane until about 1860. Then the iron versions began to make inroads until they were in almost universal use throughout the world. Stanley alone made millions of them. But like the bamboo hand-planed flyrod and its plastic counterpart, they did not completely supplant the originals in either case. Why not? Perhaps others like this author who has a complete collection of Stanley iron smooth planes – all twenty-one of them – never use them. I find them without soul, impersonal, cold, hard pushing, and almost always rusty. Enough said; let us go on with the wooden plane and its pleasurable use and construction.

A cluttered work bench

Three home-grown chiseling mallets. From left to right: Rosewood – coco bolo – lignum vitae. Two smooth planes behind them; also the handle of a turned-edge scraper rears its head. The background is filled with various files and rasps as well as a few odd chisels.

Above: **Jack planes.** From top: Two planes, both of lignum vitae; left, Brazilian tulip wood, right, maple. Below are some of the same tools, from left to right: mesquite, rosewood, lignum vitae, Brazilian tulip wood.

Opposite: **Jointer** made of lignum vitae with oak crotchwood handle.

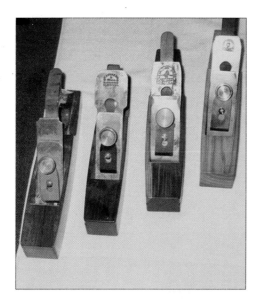

Above: A bevy of **smooth planes.** The bottom plane is of beautiful coco bolo with a white sapwood edge. The one above it is black mango from the swamps of Florida, and is also shown in close-up at left.

The smooth plane is made to the same formula as the jack plane discussed in the text, except that it is shorter – 9½ inches overall – has an integral handle – of the same shape as the handle of the jack – and has an adjustable throat piece of ¼-inch-thick brass or lignum vitae.

Opposite: A few of my diversification of **turned-edge scrapers.** Left to right: The long-handled modified bearing scraper (it is used to get pressure to scrape end wood inside the handles); half a scissor of cast steel with its turned edge running off to a point; a three-sided very useful type (these may be purchased from suppliers ready and hollow ground, needing only honing and edge-turning), along with another similar scraper; below, a handled plane blade with a concave radius for scraping curved surfaces; the straight-edge one above does large surfaces such as the coffee table upon which it is placed.

Above: **Plane wood.** From left to right, Macassar ebony, Mexican rosewood, granadilla from Central America, and tulip wood from Brazil.

Below: **A smooth plane and its parent.** The plane, including its handle, was fashioned out of a single piece of coco bolo such as the one shown.

Illustrated above is a board-room table constructed entirely by hand by the author from four book-matched mahogany planks. He used the chute board method to fit the joints of the planks, and the smooth plane and turned-edge scraper for finishing the top surface. Neither abrasive paper nor power tools went into the finishing of this project.

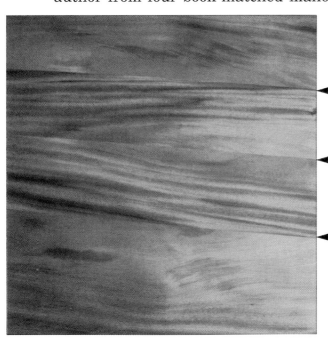

In the close-up of the table top at left, the arrows indicate the nearly invisible joinery produced by the skilled use of hand tools. Also visible are the mirror-image wood grains produced by re-sawing the original plank.

Above: **A Queen Anne tilt-top table** entirely hand made by the author of coco bolo wood from Central America. This reproduction of a 1760 family heirloom was hand cut with dovetailed legs and hand-forged latch, hand scraped and hand finished. A motorized lathe was the only power tool used.

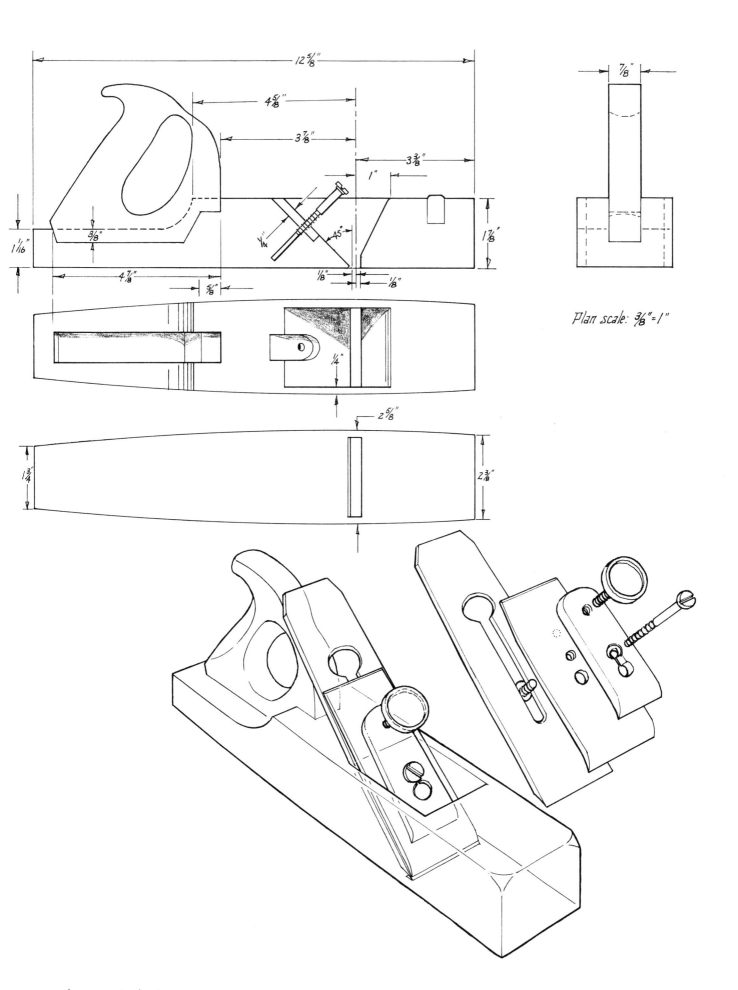

12 5/8"
4 5/8"
3 7/8"
3 3/8"
1"
45°
1/8"
3/8"
1 1/16"
4 7/8"
5/8"
1 7/8"
1/8"
1/4"
2 5/8"
1 3/4"
2 3/8"
7/8"

Plan scale: 3/8" = 1"

Cecil Pierce jack plane

Building a Wooden Plane

Let us, you and I, each build a plane together and rather simultaneously. I would like it, our first, to be the workhorse of the bench: a jack plane. For my plane I selected a piece of rosewood. Your selection of wood will of course be your own choice. In our fictitious "work-along in absentia," let's assume that my progress is always a step ahead of you. In that way, I can better carry you along.

A pleasurable and productive evening has been spent getting my piece of rosewood ready.

It measures 12⅝ inches long by 2¾ inches wide by 2 inches thick.

It is imperative that the thickness be greater than 1⅞ inches; anything less is unacceptable. It may be more, up to 2⅛ inches.

All sides and the ends are carefully squared up and made parallel to each other. Anything less will come back to haunt you. Experience has told me that.

I squared the ends up on my table saw with a smooth-cutting saw blade. They did not, and I did not expect them to, come out perfectly square. A flat single-cut file is the correction medium for this, as it will be for many other situations later on.

I straightened and smoothed the sides and top and bottom with a smooth plane and turned-edge scraper.

Lastly, using the file and scraper, I have lightly broken all corners and edges. This ensures that they do not accidentally get nicked or otherwise damaged.

After a few days away from the project, I am back at work. Even though this will be my umpteenth plane, I have the enthusiasm of a boy for the job. The wood is so beautiful, the tools so adaptable, the knowledge of pitfalls by now so infinite, and the end product so rare in this high-tech age, that there could be no more fertile seed for enthusiasm.

Having determined which side of the wood will be top and bottom, I lay it down bottom up and with my little square and a sharp pencil, draw a line across the bottom 3⅛ inches from the front end. This is a center line for the pocket and it carries around to all four sides.

The block —

Block is carefully squared and smoothed

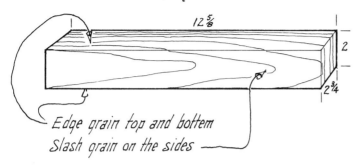

12 ⅝

2

2 ¾

Edge grain top and bottom

Slash grain on the sides

Suitable woods

beech
rock maple
apple
pecan
mesquite
lignum vitae
Vera
coco bolo
Mocassar ebony
black mango

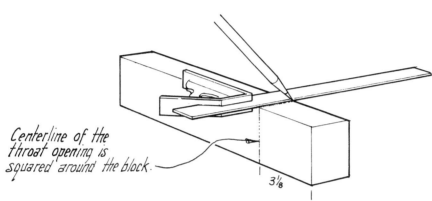

Centerline of the
throat opening is
squared around the block.

3 ⅛

Lines drawn on the block for
layout of the pocket

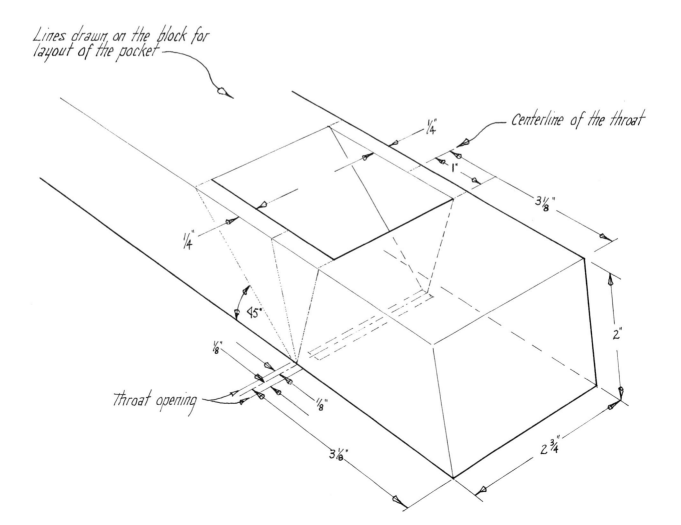

¼"

Centerline of the throat

1"

3 ⅛ "

¼"

45°

2"

⅛"

⅛"

Throat opening

3 ⅛"

2 ¾"

Next, bottom up again, I draw two more lines parallel to the center line. All with ⅛-inch spacing, one in front of and one behind the center line. This will be the throat opening.

I turn the wood top up, and 1 inch in front of the center line, I square it again. Now, I connect the front top and bottom lines on both sides of the wood and, with the wood on its side, I draw a line at 45 degrees.

This is as good a place to talk about the 45-degree business as any. This 45-degree angle is cast in stone to be the proper angle to set the iron at. Or is it?

Many years ago I talked with an old planemaker with a good reputation as such. Among other things that he said, I remember best his saying, "I always stood my irons up a little straighter in my smooth planes."

In light of the great difference in our ages, I deemed it wise not to ask him what he meant in terms of degrees. Through the years, I have tried five degrees more and five degrees less. If it matters, I am unable to detect it. Further thought supports the idea that the angle at point of contact with the wood may have the effect of standing it up straighter, because the honing angle on the flat or top side can, and usually does, alter the degrees of angle at the point of wood contact.

It is very nearly impossible to make this top perfectly flat at the edge. After honing, I use a good flat straightedge to check its truth. I hold the iron up to the north light, and you, as I, will probably be surprised at what was thought to be perfectly flat surface. But ain't.

Let's stop this digression and get back to planemaking.

Starting from the back line of the throat, draw a line at 45 degrees to the top, and do the same on the opposite side. Now draw the last line connecting the two across the top. This last will make the angle that the iron will be seated at.

With all the necessary lines in place, the next step is to chisel out the wood between them.

First, I put the piece of wood in the vise bottom up and with a, say, ¾-inch chisel, cut the area between the throat lines into a "V". In doing this, take the two lines out so that the top of the "V" is somewhat greater than ¼

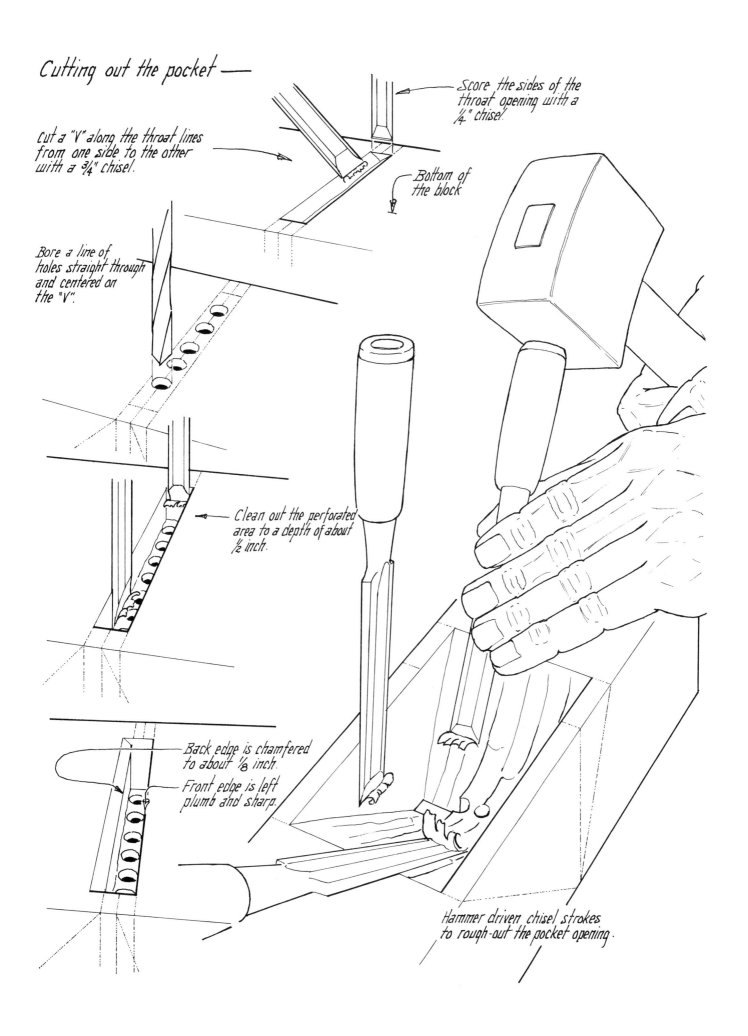

Cutting out the pocket —

Score the sides of the throat opening with a 1/4" chisel.

Cut a "V" along the throat lines from one side to the other with a 3/4" chisel.

Bottom of the block

Bore a line of holes straight through and centered on the "V".

Clean out the perforated area to a depth of about 1/2 inch.

Back edge is chamfered to about 1/8 inch.

Front edge is left plumb and sharp.

Hammer driven chisel strokes to rough-out the pocket opening.

inch. Now go to the drill press and bore a series of closely spaced holes right through to the top.

The reason for the "V" is to keep the bit or drill from lifting up splinters from the bottom wood.

Perhaps this is a good time to counsel the uninitiated that this cutting-out of the wood is the most critical operation in the entire project. Chip the bottom edges and there is no remedy. Chip the top edges and you can probably live with it – so "careful" is a very important word.

With a brad-point bit in the chuck and the plane bottom-up and lying on a piece of scrap wood (this latter to insure there is no chipping when the bit goes through) – the plane pocket has been pierced. In doing this boring, we must not violate the wood of the ¼-inch sidewalls.

I bore my first hole about ½ inch from the edge, then measure if it comes through the top at the same distance. Then I feel secure that all is well and that I am boring straight.

With the plane back in the drill vise, still bottom up, this whole perforated area is chiseled down about ½ inch vertical on front and sides, slanting on the back side. I will use a ½-inch chisel and ¼ inch for the sides. You use what is comfortable for you. My wood is very hard, yours may be softer, therefore you could use larger tools.

The size of the chisel, timewise, will not make much difference. I expect to use up two long evenings before the job is cut out and cleaned up. This last cutting-down was to ensure that the chisel coming down from the top does not come down on thin wood of the bottom and split or chip it out. This has gone along much faster with the pen than with the chisel.

Now the plane turns over in the vise — of course we have a thick piece of scrap wood in the bottom of the vise, bringing the work well above the vise top —

Oh, I forgot to tell you that before I turned over in the vise, the back edge of the chiseled throat was chamfered back, square with the slanting bed, about ⅛". This chamfer will be maintained in the finished plane.

I feel sure that you have gotten by the chiseling-out from the bottom and are now ready to turn it top side up for chiseling out from the top.

You have four lines previously drawn to confine and define your work.

Smoothing the pocket —

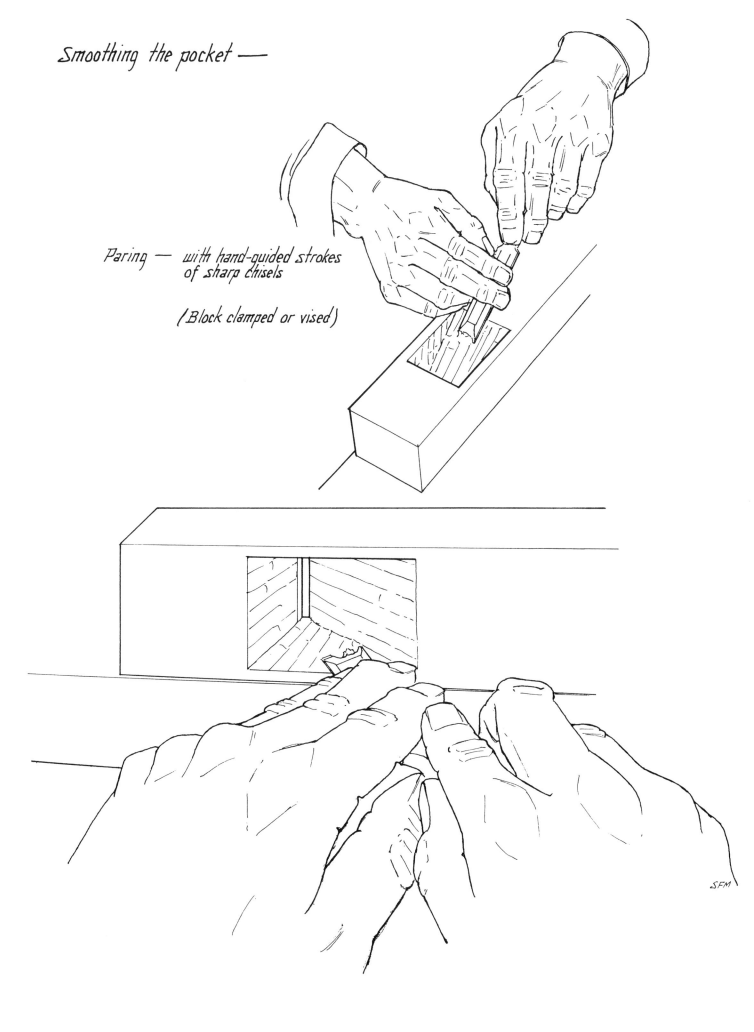

Paring — with hand-guided strokes
of sharp chisels

(Block clamped or vised)

SFM

Again chipping and splitting are a hazard. Again do the work, as before, with a chisel whose size you are comfortable with.

I chiseled carefully and not too deeply an outlining groove on all four sides, leaving the lines intact.

The second time around, I worked deeper into the wood. From there on I was able to cut out satisfying chips.

There seems to be no way to keep the 45-degree slope and the vertical sidewalls vertical except following some inner sense. The forward slope is in no way critical. As I cannot look in on your work, I shall assume that you have finished the chiseling and have followed my warnings.

There is excess rather than a lack of wood on the sides and slope which needs to be removed. Perhaps I should say right here that the inner sidewall and forward slope should be as smooth and polished as their counterparts outside. Frankly, I am never satisfied that I have achieved this goal. But I strive for it!

How do we proceed?

First, here are the tools that I work with. A thick sharp paring chisel, a #50 and a #49 Nicholson cabinet rasp, several sizes and shapes of floats, an array of files both coarse and fine. Many kinds and shapes of turned-edge scrapers and a good sharp knife.

Who has all of these tools?

Let's get more practical for our first plane. For my early planes and my not-so-early ones also, I had the paring chisel, some files and a knife, that is it. I pared, I filed and I scraped with the knife.

Although they are expensive, one should have a #50 Nicholson rasp. It does so many things well and cannot be beat for working out the handle that lies ahead in this project.

Now the next step is to either install the iron or the handle. My choice is the iron because it extends up above the handle and it is preferable to fit the handle afterwards. This avoids possible interference of the handle with the top of the iron.

The screw, which is modified from a wood screw of either stainless steel or silicon bronze (any other material is not strong enough), is installed exactly central sidewise and to the other dimensions as set forth in the drawings.

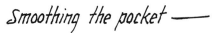
Smoothing the pocket ——

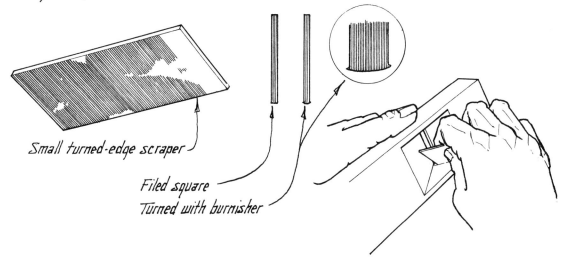

Small turned-edge scraper

Filed square
Turned with burnisher

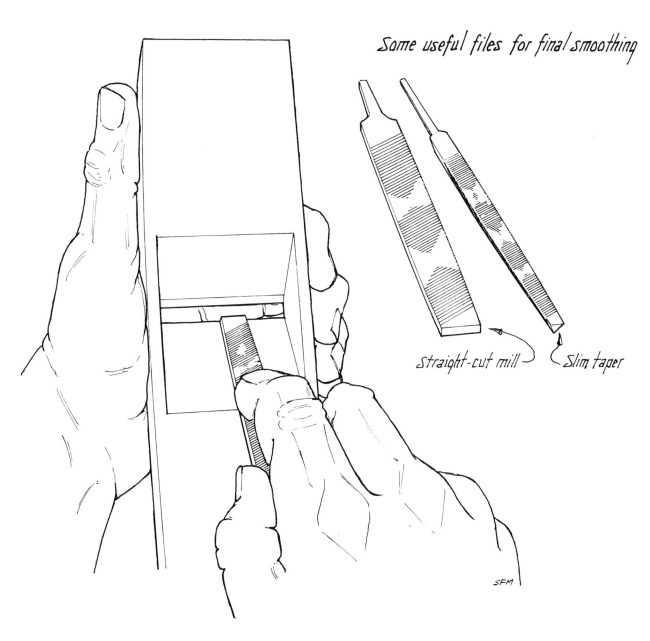

Some useful files for final smoothing

Straight-cut mill — Slim taper

SFM

Cutting the block to final dimensions ———

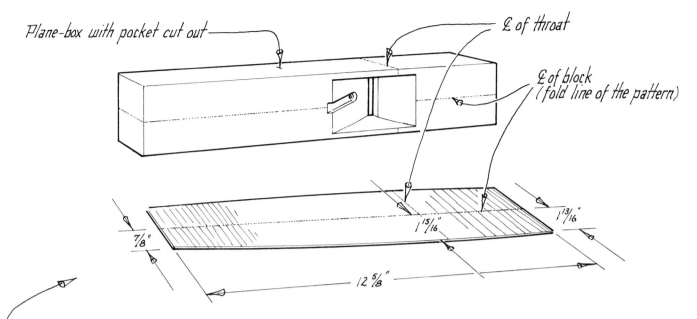

Plane-box with pocket cut out ———

℄ of throat

℄ of block
(fold line of the pattern)

1¹³⁄₁₆"

1¹⁵⁄₁₆"

⅞"

12⅝"

Paper template for bottom and top of the box oriented to the longitudinal centerline (℄) of the carefully squared block and to the athwartships ℄ of the plane's throat. Cut one side in a "fair" curve through the offsets shown. Fold the paper, mark and cut the opposite side.

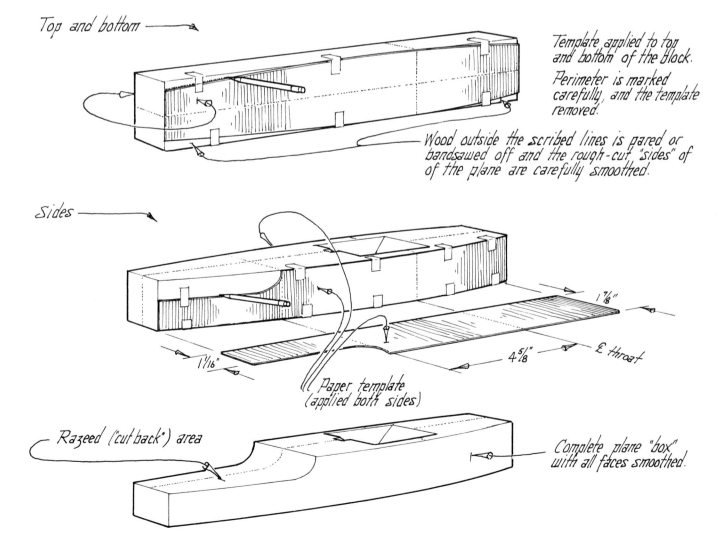

Top and bottom ———

Template applied to top and bottom of the block.

Perimeter is marked carefully, and the template removed.

Wood outside the scribed lines is pared or bandsawed off and the rough-cut "sides" of of the plane are carefully smoothed.

Sides ———

1⁷⁄₈"

1¹⁄₁₆"

4⅝"

℄ throat

Paper template
(applied both sides)

Razeed ("cutback") area

Complete plane "box" with all faces smoothed.

The proper drill size for #16 screw, in hardwood, is #9 at .196 diameter.

I assume that, in addition to reading my running comments and then perhaps becoming lost in the maze of it, you are also studying the accompanying drawings for further clarity.

We are now at a crossroad. We have a nice piece of wood all chiselled out and cleaned up. But it needs the iron installed and a handle.

Let me step backward here and tell you that I kept the throat in the bottom as narrow as possible but did not warn you to do likewise. Later, we will properly enlarge it.

Assuming that you are following my lead, you will need to know how to modify the iron and chip breaker, or double iron as it is sometimes known, so that they, as a unit, will go down over the head of the big screw.

All is drawn in detail but here also are my details.

First, the very bottom of the slot must be enlarged, either by drilling or grinding with a hand-held grinder, until the ⁷⁄₁₆" head of the screw will freely enter through it.

Now with the chip breaker screwed to the iron in its normal position, put it in the drill press with the chip breaker down. Using the enlarged slot as a guide, drill a ⁷⁄₁₆" hole in the chip breaker. This hole is to be positioned below, as close as practicable, but clearing the head of the large binding screw.

Now we need a toggle to hold the above unit in place and to hold it securely.

First, I will tell you how to make it yourself as I did my first ones which were of steel.

If you do not have a metal lathe you may easily replace it with a ⁵⁄₁₆" S.A.E. cap screw, the head of which can be slotted for a screwdriver. Do not use a wrench to tighten it, as the big screw is not intended to assume so much pressure.

The counter bored hole can be managed also by making a counter bore, which can be properly ground from any ⁷⁄₁₆" drill, even a worn-out one.

Another answer to this problem may be to purchase from me a kit consisting of the bronze toggle, a bronze thumb wheel, plus a bronze big screw, all of which are fully machined for the job.

Fitting the iron to the block ——

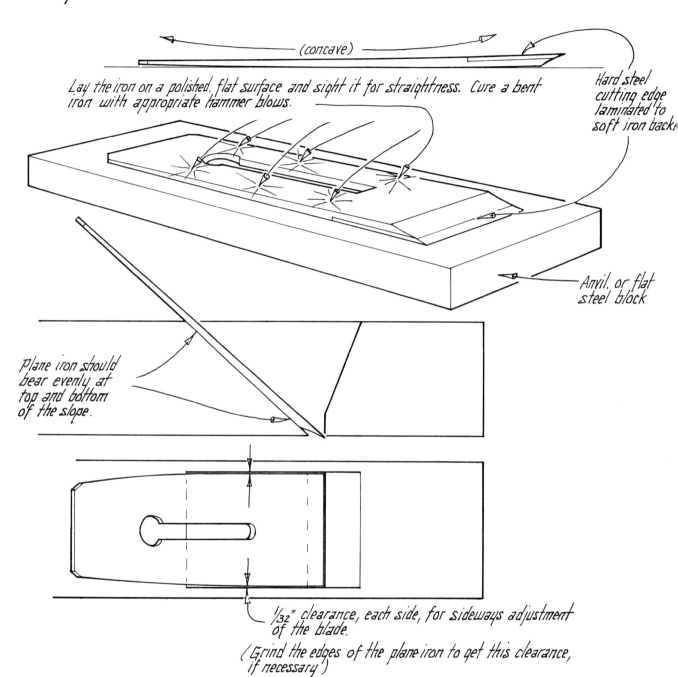

(concave)

Hard steel cutting edge laminated to soft iron back

Lay the iron on a polished, flat surface and sight it for straightness. Cure a bent iron with appropriate hammer blows.

Anvil, or flat steel block

Plane iron should bear evenly at top and bottom of the slope.

$\frac{1}{32}$" clearance, each side, for sideways adjustment of the blade.

(Grind the edges of the plane iron to get this clearance, if necessary.)

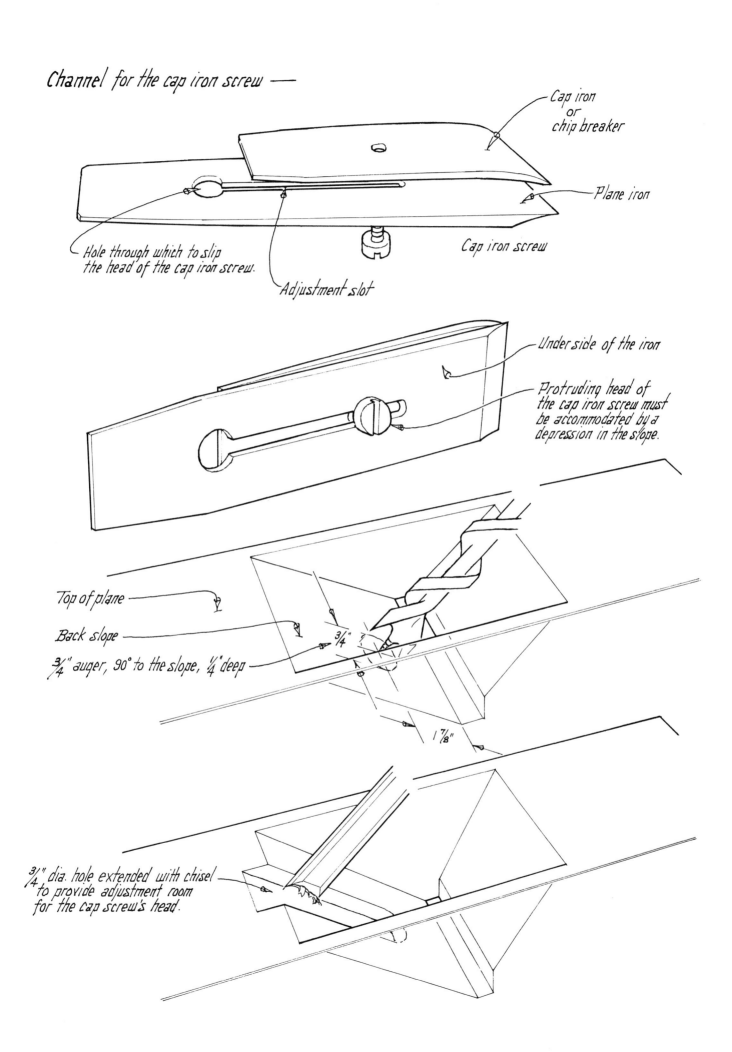

Channel for the cap iron screw —

Cap iron
or
chip breaker

Plane iron

Hole through which to slip
the head of the cap iron screw.

Adjustment slot

Cap iron screw

Under side of the iron

Protruding head of
the cap iron screw must
be accommodated by a
depression in the slope.

Top of plane

Back slope

$\frac{3}{4}$" auger, 90° to the slope, $\frac{1}{4}$" deep

$\frac{3}{4}$"

$1\frac{7}{8}$"

$\frac{3}{4}$" dia. hole extended with chisel
to provide adjustment room
for the cap screw's head.

The pressure-holding screw —

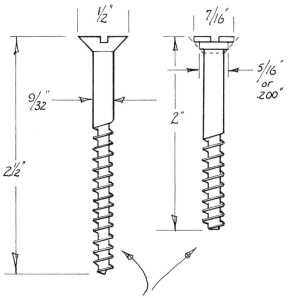

½"

7/16"

9/32"

5/16"
or
.200"

2"

2½"

2½" #16 stainless steel or Everdur bronze screw,
cut off and machined to provide a 5/16" swelled
collar under the head.

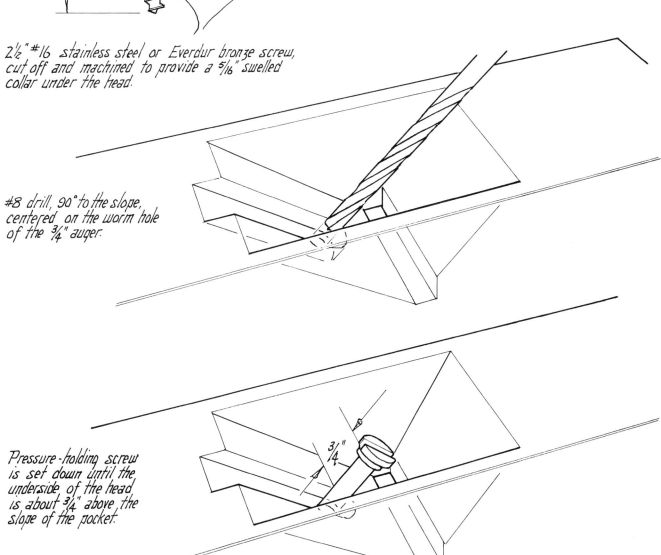

#8 drill, 90° to the slope,
centered on the worm hole
of the ¾" auger.

Pressure-holding screw
is set down until the
underside of the head
is about ¾" above the
slope of the pocket.

¾"

Modifying the chip breaker to receive the pressure screw —

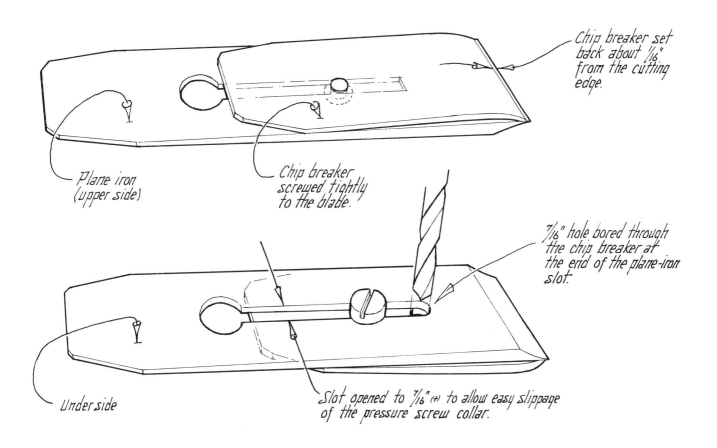

Chip breaker set back about ¹/₁₆" from the cutting edge.

Plane iron (upper side)

Chip breaker screwed tightly to the blade.

⁷/₁₆" hole bored through the chip breaker at the end of the plane-iron slot.

Underside

Slot opened to ⁷/₁₆"(+) to allow easy slippage of the pressure screw collar.

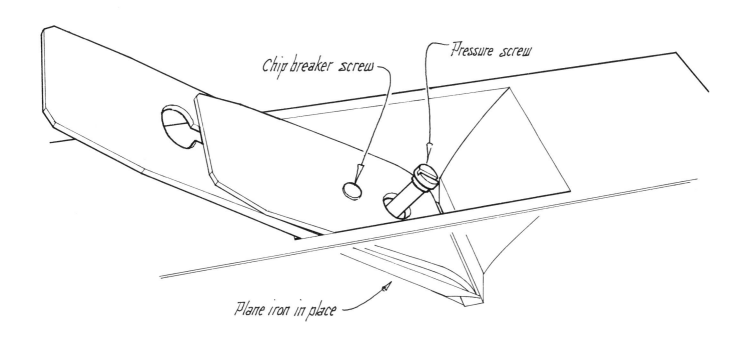

Chip breaker screw

Pressure screw

Plane iron in place

Here, let me tell you why the toggle instead of the timeless wedge.

To adjust any wooden plane's iron with a hammer, the iron is tapped lightly down, and a rather short rap on the strike button will bring it back up. This last is the doom of the wedge system because it also at the same time loosens the wedge, which is exasperating to say the least. The same would happen to the toggle but the counter bore prohibits it, causing a downward push. Other attempts to adjust the iron have been made with, more or less modern, hermaphroditical means such as a screw adjustment which is doubtful of accuracy in increments .001-.002 of an inch.

The above takes care of the iron. It is now easily and quickly mounted or removed from the plane. Now we remove it and put aside for a while.

We are ready to razee the back end. This is very important, for not only does it professionalize the plane aesthetically but it puts the hand low and behind the iron. Were the hand too high, it would waste the exertion by causing a downward push, creating additional friction.

To me and many others, any plane not razeed is misshapen, unlovely, even ugly — in shop language, a "wooden world" or a "clunker."

As you might suspect, my plane is finished, but I am carrying on for instruction's sake. No longer can the handle be ignored.

It is rather difficult to do well. So relax, have a smoke or whatever you do while I tell you this story, which is somewhat germane to what is ahead.

My quest for knowledge in anything I do makes me a candidate for many adventures, often wild-goose chases, even though my subconscious tells me they should be ignored.

An ad in a woodworking magazine caught my eye. It was for a videotape about how to make a wooden plane.

"Hey!" I thought, "this may be just the thing, it may turn over some stones that I missed and there may be a nugget beneath."

So off went my check for forty dollars or so in the following mail. Some time later, when the mailman delivered it, I was like a child at Christmas, leaving my work and going immediately to it. After viewing the preliminary warning of the penalties for copying, etc., an elderly gentleman came on and held forth on the desirability of the wooden plane and what was to follow.

The toggle ——

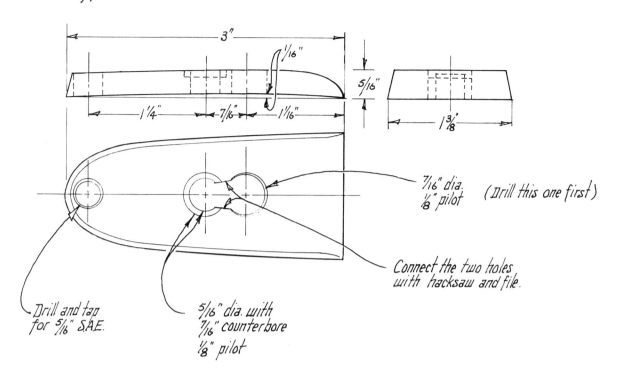

3"

1/16"

5/16"

1 1/4"   7/16"   1 1/16"

1 3/8"

7/16" dia.
1/8" pilot   (Drill this one first)

Connect the two holes
with hacksaw and file.

Drill and tap
for 5/16" S.A.E.

5/16" dia. with
7/16" counterbore
1/8" pilot

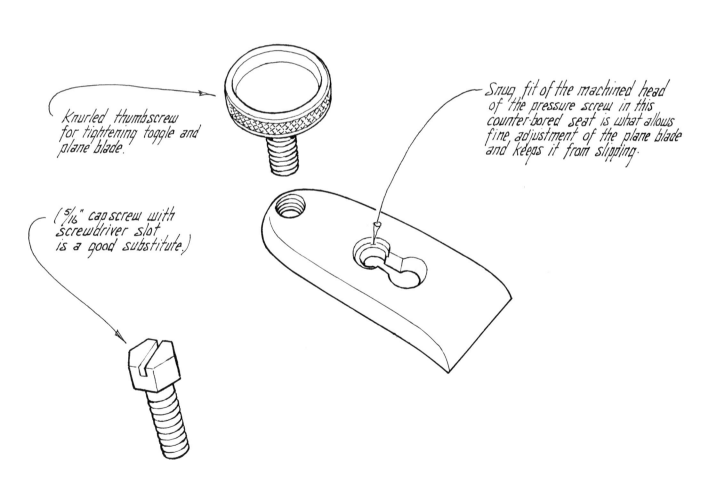

Knurled thumbscrew
for tightening toggle and
plane blade.

(5/16" cap screw with
screwdriver slot
is a good substitute.)

Snug fit of the machined head
of the pressure screw in this
counter-bored seat is what allows
fine adjustment of the plane blade
and keeps it from slipping.

His remarks were brief and soon I was viewing a workman in a shop so sterile that it could have been a lab at the local hospital. No errant chip or shaving marred the floor or factory-made craftsman's bench. Likewise, no crude tools such as chisels, rasps, or a mallet graced the unworn top of that bench. Panning around, I was introduced to an array of top-of-the-line power tools; some like the horizontal boring machine were new to me.

It turned out that he was not going to need any hand tools, for the plane was going to be made of three pieces of wood, all precisely machined, then dowelled and glued together. I had gone through and abandoned that phase half a lifetime ago.

My enthusiasm for learning something here had disappeared. But I kept on watching, trying to get my forty dollars' worth by gloating to myself. I wanted to determine how this craftsman was going to make the handle with these power tools alone.

The show in due time progressed to the stage where the tool was operable, and he put a piece of what appeared to be white pine in the vise and produced a few shavings from it. He then held the tool aloft for the camcorder and announced that the tool was done and that a plane did not need a handle anyway.

A redeeming feature for me was that after all he used the thing conventionally — he didn't pull the plane toward him and had he used a saw, he probably wouldn't have pulled that either.

I'm old-fashioned and follow in the ways that I was taught, hoping they will not die in usage.

We have advanced to the point where a handle is needed.

Consult the drawing and lay out on a piece of thin pattern wood the contours. This will be much better to work from than to lay out directly on the handle stock.

Leave excess wood on the bottom. It will be useful to hold the piece by in the vise. I sawed mine out on the bandsaw and with a Forstner bit bored out, roughly, the hand hole.

Anything goes in finishing up the handle, even abrasive paper rolled into a tight roll. Jackknife, various rasps and files, any special scrapers, all have

The handle — cutting out and rounding — (hand tools assumed)

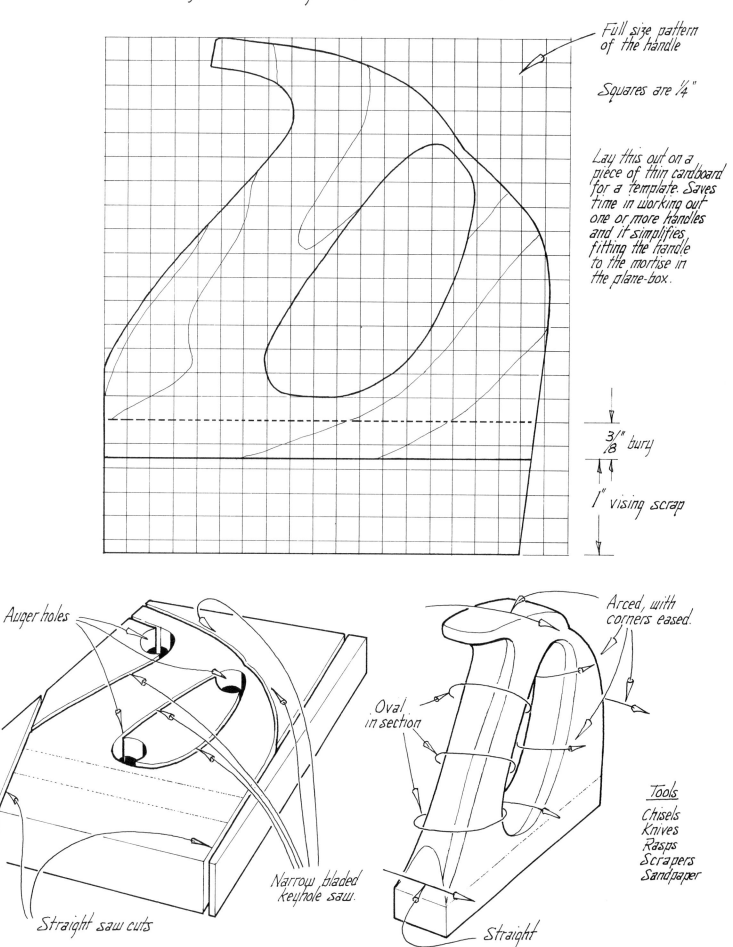

Full size pattern of the handle

Squares are 1/4"

Lay this out on a piece of thin cardboard for a template. Saves time in working out one or more handles and it simplifies fitting the handle to the mortise in the plane-box.

$\frac{3}{8}$" bury

1" vising scrap

Auger holes

Straight saw cuts

Narrow bladed keyhole saw.

Arced, with corners eased.

Oval in section

Straight

Tools

Chisels
Knives
Rasps
Scrapers
Sandpaper

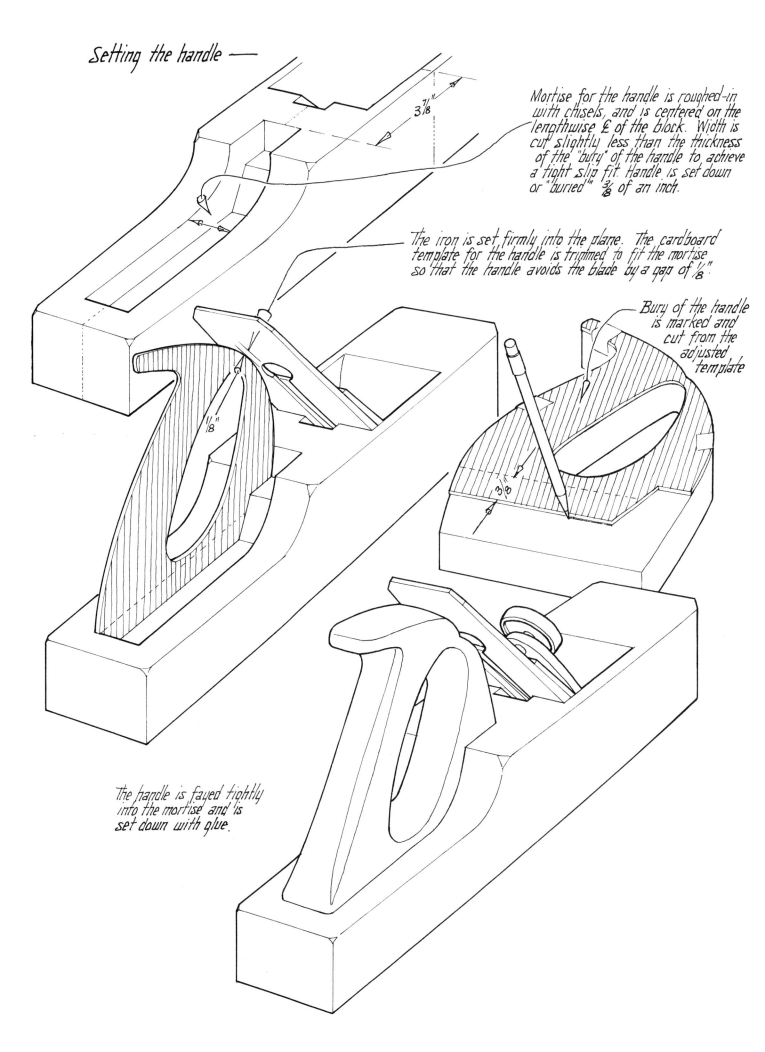

Setting the handle —

$3\frac{7}{8}"$

Mortise for the handle is roughed-in
with chisels, and is centered on the
lengthwise ℄ of the block. Width is
cut slightly less than the thickness
of the "bury" of the handle to achieve
a tight slip fit. Handle is set down
or "buried" $\frac{3}{8}$ of an inch.

The iron is set firmly into the plane. The cardboard
template for the handle is trimmed to fit the mortise
so that the handle avoids the blade by a gap of $\frac{1}{8}"$.

Bury of the handle
is marked and
cut from the
adjusted
template

$\frac{1}{8}"$

$3\frac{3}{8}"$

The handle is fayed tightly
into the mortise and is
set down with glue.

their use here. It took me a long evening to work out mine.

Assuming that you have a cut-out razee on the back end of the plane and a finished handle, this is how you put them together.

With the plane held upright in the vise having the iron in place, hold the handle on the side of the plane that is away from you, with front side of the handle clearing the iron by about ⅛ inch and at an angle that seems about right.

Draw a line on the side of the handle using the contour of the razee as a guide. Take it down and add ⅜ of an inch to this line, and bandsaw to the last line.

You are now ready to mark by the bottom of the handle and chisel out a mortise in the plane to receive it. After chiseling the mortise in the plane down ⅜ of an inch, the plane is ready to receive the handle. I bedded mine in epoxy resin.

Sharpening the Iron

Our book contains no more important section than this one, for without proper sharpening of the iron our wooden plane will not be the superior tool that we wish it to be.

The goal in the first step of sharpening, both the plane iron and the chisel, is to produce a hollowed-out bevel. The knowledge of doing this goes back in time, at least, to Moxon. Joseph Moxon, writing in the late 1600s in his book *Mechanicle Exercises,* says (using modern spelling):

> When you grind your iron, place your two thumbs under the iron, and your fingers of both hands upon the iron, and so clap down your iron to the stone, holding it to that angle with the stone you intend the basil (bezel, bevel) shall have: Keep the iron in this posture, without either mounting, or sinking its ends all the while the stone is turning about; and when you lift the iron off the stone, to see if it is ground to your mind; if it be not, you must be sure you place the iron again in the same position on the stone that it had before; or else you will make a double basil on your iron: But if it be true set on the stone and steadily kept to that position, your basil will be hollow, and the smaller your grindstone is, the hollower it will be. You may know when it is well ground by the evenness, and entireness of the edge all the way.
>
> Having ground your iron, you must smoothen the edge finer with a good whet-stone. Thus, hold the edge of your iron upwards in your left hand, and your whet-stone in your right and having first spit upon your stone to whet it, apply it to the basil of your iron. In such a position that it may bear upon the whole breadth of the basil and so working the stone over the basil, you will quickly wear the coarser grating of the grind-stone off the edge of that side. Then turn the flat side of the iron, and apply the stone flat to it, till you have worn off the coarse gratings of the grindstone on that side too.

So wrote Moxon on his method of hollow grinding, which is the bedrock upon which all sharpening is, or should be, built.

He did, however, fail to mention that an accomplice was necessary to turn the grindstone with a hand crank, and to keep water copiously pouring on the revolving stone.

Such was my job as a boy when my father needed to sharpen his axe or scythe. And spitting on the whetstone was the norm in my early days also.

But Benny Rand, the premier boatbuilder of our area, used the wonderful new stone called an oilstone upon which he poured kerosene. Father always used to take the opportunity, when we visited the shop, to sharpen his pocketknife on the oilstone. I ached to follow his action but knew, without asking, that a mere boy with an old castoff jackknife in his hip pocket was off limits to that sacred oilstone.

Right here I believe that we should say some more about tool steel and to do this, let us turn back to where I said of cast steel, "This is the finest steel ever produced to take and hold a keen edge for the working of wood by hand tools."

I want to modify this statement. The easy way would be to go back to the computer and just do it, but that would not tell the reason. Even as I write, changes in technologies are influencing my methods.

Mr. Carl Dorsch published, in the spring issue of *Woodwork* magazine, his article entitled "The Cutting Edge of Tool Steels." Mr. Dorsch seems eminently qualified to write on the subject, being a tool research engineer in Pittsburgh, Pennsylvania, the cradle of steel U.S.A. He goes into a brief and interesting history of tool steel-making in which he mentions mushet.

If you remember, I also mentioned mushet back along. Before I discuss Dorsch's comments on tool steel, I will digress and tell you about my introduction to mushet.

During the Second World War I did some defense work, as it was called, in two small shops. In one shop I made aircraft parts, employing patriotic but untrained men and women for help. The parts were threads in several fine thread sizes + 2 inches long to class three fits, which was an extremely close tolerance. Headaches?!!

In the other shop we did general machine work, using two long-retired machinists and a summer-vacationing school principal.

One of the retired machinists was Lyman Fisher. Whenever our high-speed tool bits would not seem to do well in some particularly hard metal, Lyman would lament, "Oh, if I only had some mushet."

It meant nothing to me then. But as I look back now and read about mushet, Lyman may have been on the right track.

He was a fine worker and whenever Lyman was boring a long hole he stood at the lathe with his hand on the tool post always. One day I asked him why he did this. His answer was that he could not hear when the tool had gone through the cut but that he could feel the vibration, or lack of it.

Robert Mushet (1811-1891) was the son of a Scottish ironmaster. They were both experimenters. In the latter part of his life Robert happened on a process of steelmaking which gave the world "R. Mushet's Special Steel." It set records all over the industrialized world, especially the United States, for heavy feeds and high speed in metal working. Mushet saw fit not to patent his process but to produce it secretly, going to great lengths to buy and deliver the Wolfram ore and other ingredients in a clandestine manner. When he died he took the process with him. It may have been better than H.S.S. For more on Mushet, see F. M. Osborne's *The Story of the Mushets* (London: Nelson, 1952).

Lyman, in later years, gave me a piece of mushet but in my youthful enthusiasm my attempts to use it did not turn out well. He probably used this metal at the old Bath Iron Works in Bath, Maine.

Before I reminisced about those war years, I was going to modify my statement about "cast steel" being the best. I hereby modify my previous statement by adding the words, "the best that is reasonably available."

It would be strange indeed if a hundred years of tool steel making had not come up with a better product. Though there is a recent superior tool steel, Mr. Dorsch's instructions on how to proceed to acquire some of this new steel make it impossible for the common toolmaker to obtain it. It is unlikely that a planemaker or user would ever be successful in the quest. Therefore my statement, with the modification, still stands and I defend it.

Now, there is a truism which I want to pass on to you. It goes like this: "The most versatile of all tools is the human hand, but it is weak and it is fallible." It is especially pertinent to that which follows.

I have made what are, to me at least, some exciting strides in quality of and speed in sharpening. Some are my own and some borrowed from others. We are going to sharpen with simple jigs or error-free holding devices and diamond.

I can just hear your thoughts as you read this: "What kind of person is this? He starts out touting the making and using of the wooden plane; now he turns to the high tech of using diamond to sharpen them!"

Perhaps this story will let you into this ancient brain and how it works. I am a member of a woodworking club named the Kennebec Valley Woodworking Association. We hold monthly night meetings at different members' shops.

A while ago, maybe a year, I carried with me a piece of what had been, a few hours earlier, green-wood white birch, about 2" x 2" x 10". It had been put through my microwave about six short cycles. It was completely dry and had no cracks.

No one, it appeared including me, was greatly impressed. The whole thing was forgotten by me until a recent meeting when a member came bringing a piece of maple about three or four inches square.

He had turned a bowl on one end of it but had not yet severed it from the parent stock. He had, he said, started with green wood and cured it in the micro. He worried that it was not dry enough and might yet crack. What to do now?

Some members had answers varying from more micro to burying it in sawdust. To this last, I interjected that if he buried it in sawdust he need not look for results any time soon.

After the meeting was adjourned, Roy called me to one side and said, "Cecil, I thought you were for the old methods."

Not knowing just what he was driving at (this was all in good nature), I said, "Why yes, Roy, that seems accurate."

"Well then, how come you don't want to dry wood in sawdust, an old and proven way, but you want to do it in a microwave!?"

Herein lies my psychology. If it is proven better in a predominant way, then I buy it, even Mr. Dorsch's tool steel. Very likely, a honed edge, the equal of the diamond-produced one, can be obtained by the use of black hard Arkansas stone, but at a cost in comparative time that I consider prohibitive.

At the beginning of this section I wrote about the venerated hollow bevel on the cutting edge of the iron. Now I want to write about producing this hollow bevel quickly, accurately, and with a fixture or jig, if you will, that anyone can make from materials found in any shop, given that a common bench grinder is available. Indebtedness for this following design goes to friend, neighbor, and master craftsman, Maurice Sherman.

For many years my own method was to simply stand to the grinder without any guide at all. Doing it so much I developed a "feel" for putting it back to the wheel, after constantly dipping it in water to cool it, inspecting the progress, and finding the same groove.

This served me quite well but there was a void. I needed a better method, a way to remove the "fallibility of the human hand" as in the quoted truism.

The machinist in me could only think in terms of precision slides and cross slides and precision grinding head.

I built one along these lines. It performed well enough, in fact beautifully, producing a grind unnecessarily accurate, considering that it was going to be finally hand honed.

While this was going on, this book, and this chapter in particular, was being worked up in my mind. How was I going to explain and suggest that a reader develop a clone of this grinder?

Expressing my dilemma to Maurice, he said, "Why don't you come and see how I do it?"

Now his shop is no stranger to me, but somehow this had escaped me. When he demonstrated to me what he had built out of white pine scrap, a piece of one-half-inch copper water tubing, and a couple of stove bolts, I knew that his was the best possible answer to the problem.

I came home and built one immediately. My scrap pile, however, pro-

Guide rail —

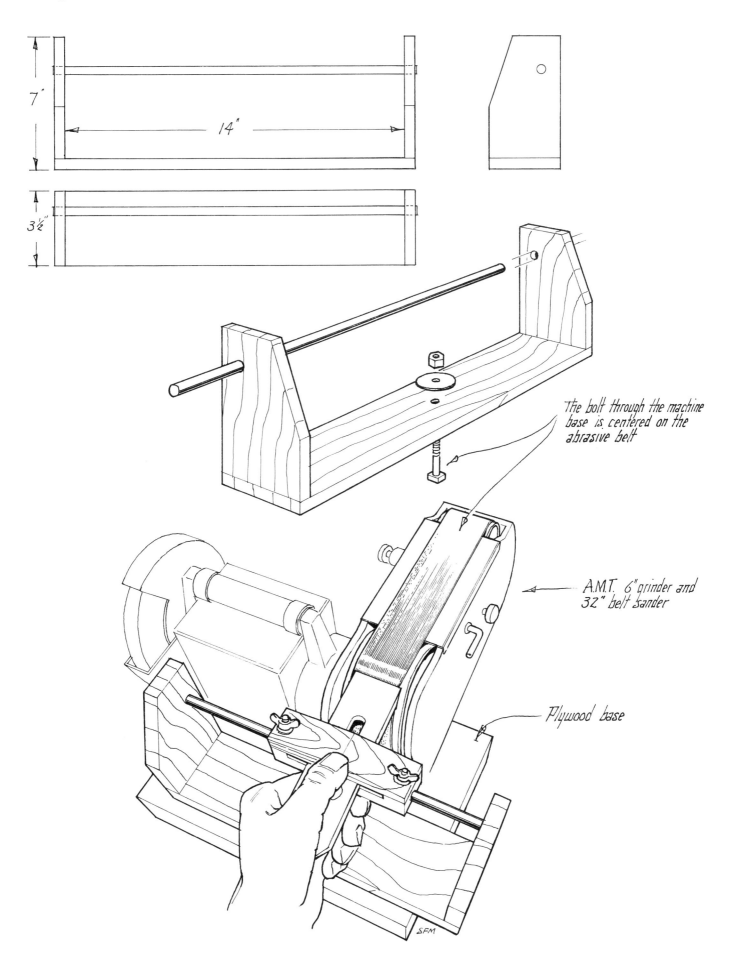

7"

14"

3½"

The bolt through the machine base is centered on the abrasive belt

A.M.T. 6" grinder and 32" belt sander

Plywood base

SFM

The guide-rider —

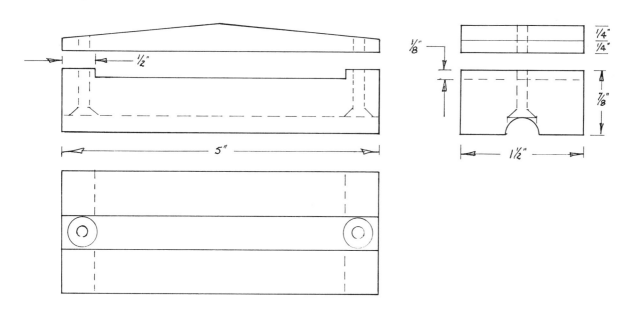

$\frac{1}{2}$"

$\frac{1}{8}$"

$\frac{1}{4}$"
$\frac{1}{4}$"

$\frac{7}{8}$"

5"

$1\frac{1}{2}$"

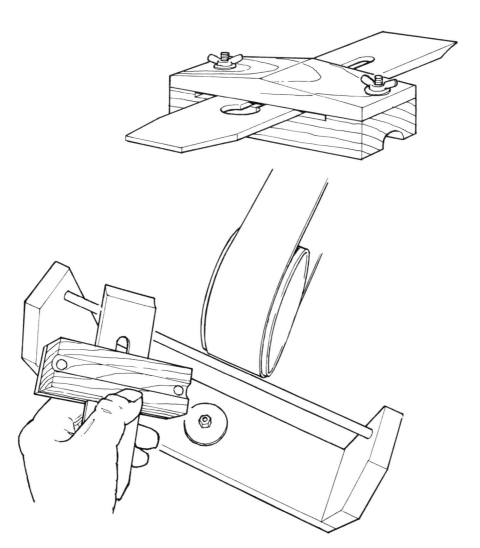

duced black walnut for the frame, rosewood for the shuttle, and stainless tubing for the shuttle bar. For all this, mine works no better than does Maurice's of white pine.

This fixture works equally well used on either a grinding wheel or belt grinder. Mine is used on a belt grinder.

While all this was going on, a catalog came in the bulk mail from American Machine & Tool Co. in Royersford, Penn. Upon perusal it proved to have a new grinder – belt sander – that appeared heaven-sent for my tool grinding. The price seemed right and I bought one.

The belt grinding of tools creates much less heat than wheel grinding, sometimes needing no dipping in water at all.

The machine is very versatile. For instance, a friend brought in two axes which appeared to have cut as much gravel as wood. Would I sharpen them? Of course, a person who uses axes these days deserves to have them sharp.

Knowing how difficult it is to get a dull axe down to edge on a bench grinding wheel, I tried putting the grinding belt in the vertical mode with a coarse grit belt. It just ate those axes up, and in no time at all they were down to a honing edge. I highly recommend this machine.

Now let me take you to what is really exciting, to me at least. I could always, in some manner, get a reasonably effective hollow grind on the basil (Moxon) or bevel. Honing the edge to the ultimate sharpness was something else.

My indebtedness is to Mr. Allan Boardman of California for telling me that he used diamond compound for the honing medium. It was like the quarterback had passed me the ball. You find your own way to the end zone for a touchdown. It was a long run.

Allan had said, "Ask the knifemakers, they know all about diamond honing."

My first act was to phone the only knifemaker that I know of. It was all news to him; he used aluminum oxide.

Surely my machine-shop suppliers in Boston would have it.

No luck, nor did they know of anyone who did.

I happened to have, in the back reaches of a tool chest, part of a tube of

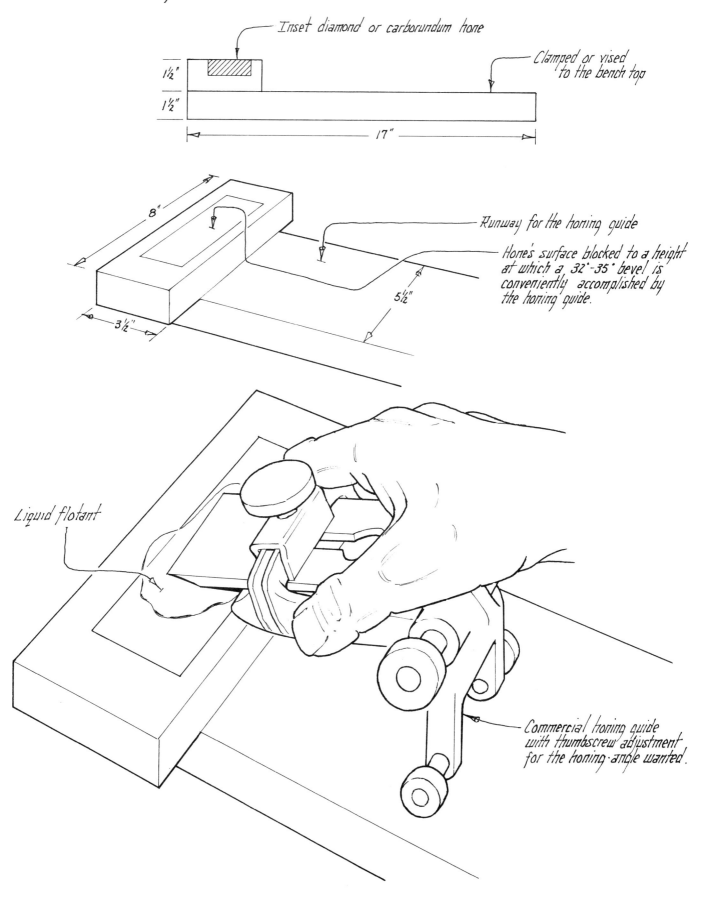

Portable honing station —

Inset diamond or carborundum hone

Clamped or vised to the bench top

1½"

1½"

17"

8"

3½"

5½"

Runway for the honing guide

Hone's surface blocked to a height at which a 32°-35° bevel is conveniently accomplished by the honing guide.

Liquid flotant

Commercial honing guide with thumbscrew adjustment for the honing-angle wanted.

Wooden substitute for a commercial honing guide —

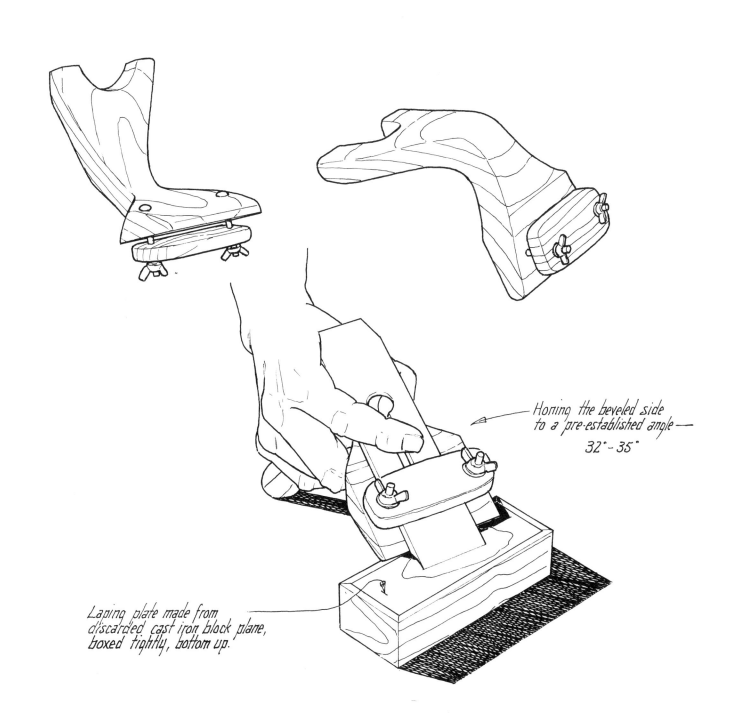

Horing the beveled side
to a pre-established angle —
32° - 35°

Laping plate made from
discarded cast iron block plane,
boxed tightly, bottom up.

the stuff. It is packaged in a plastic hypodermic-type dispenser. I had bought it at a used tool establishment against the time that I might have a use for it.

Returning to this tube and its box I found a hitherto unnoticed address: Elgin Diamond Products, 366 Bluff City Blvd., Elgin, Illinois 60120.

My letter to them asked if I could buy from them directly. They answered me back by telephone! Yes, they would sell to me, but preferred to sell through their sales representatives.

My representative would be the New England one: Ipsco Industrial Services, P. O. Box 295, Attleboro, Massachusetts 02703. Toll-free number: 1-800-642-4044.

While I had Elgin on the phone, I improved the occasion to gain some knowledge, especially the grading specifications.

That which I already had was grade #9, this being too coarse for the purpose.

He said #9 was 1800 grit – #3, 8000 grit – #1, the finest, 14000!

He asked me what it was being used for? When told honing of woodworking tools, it surprised him. When I commented that Allan said he used size 1 micron, he was surprised again, as this was the finest grade.

He suggested size #3, which is 8000 grit. This size I bought, only to find it to be also on the coarse side.

Eventually buying #1 or 1 micron, I found it was perfect, proving Allan to be correct.

While on the subject of diamond: Very recently the Wall Street Journal had a front-page article on the subject. Here I want to share the pertinent areas of the article with you.

The story deals with the alleged possibility that a person had pilfered the recipe for making industrial diamonds from General Electric, even though the plant is guarded like Fort Knox, or so they thought. The article points out that the ingredients for making synthetic diamond are rather well known. But like our Mushet Steel, the cooking of it is the secret.

Also quoted is Prof. John Angus of Case Western Reserve University: "Diamond has properties that are duplicated by no other material. It is harder than anything, stronger than anything, conducts heat better than anything. I mean anything."

Having taken care of the hollowing-out with fixtures of our own making, now to use this diamond honing we have to purchase some items, namely, a fine grit (600) diamond whetstone.

D.M.T. is a good choice but any 600 grit will do. You may even use any natural or man-made stone that you may have. But this will be much slower and less accurate as these stones do not stay flat.

Next, again, to eliminate the fallibility of the human hand you will need a sharpening guide from Woodcraft in Woburn, Mass.

There are several offered, but get the one that is hinged in the middle and has the roller on the back end. — I modified mine by putting a longer axle in so that the wheels could be on the outside, making it more stable — but it is very usable as it comes to you.

Finally, a tube of Elgin's diamond lapping compound, ¾ oz. size grade 1 STRG. This is not as expensive as you might expect, in the neighborhood of $15.00 per tube.

To get this all together so that you can cook with it, you will need to make what I shall call a portable honing station (refer to the illustration for details and use).

The base for this is laminated hardwood – maple is fine – my first one – solid 1½" wood – quickly acquired an unacceptable warp. It ended its short life as firewood.

You will need a cast-iron lapping plate. They are too expensive to buy as such. Mine is made using the bottom of an old Stanley block plane, not the narrow ones but the wider the better. These are perfect for the job because the metal is old and therefore stabilized by age. It was flat when made, but you won't find it to be now. It will have to be worked. We tend to think of metal as staying as it was machined. Nothing could be farther from the truth. Your old plane bottom will prove to have low places up to .002 or .003. Unacceptable!

The Swede, C. E. Johannson, who made the first high-precision gauge blocks, said his biggest problem was not producing the extreme accuracy but getting the metal at rest. I worked mine flat by the Prussian blue and hand scraper method. This method is as old as time and still viable. You may want to go to your friendly machine shop to have it precision ground.

Assuming that we have the portable work station, we mount upon one end, the left-hand one, the D.M.T. sharpening stone or any other 600 grit diamond sharpening device. This mounting will be permanent and at an arbitrary height of 1½ inches above the work station base.

Also assuming that we have a flat cast-iron lapping plate, we build this up to the same 1½-inch height as the aforementioned permanent stone.

This and all subsequent "stones" should be of the universal height, and besides the lone permanent one, all others should be movable at will upon the station base. Also all these movable stones should have coarse abrasive paper bottoms which will prevent their movement when in use.

These cast-iron laps will need to be scored on their working surfaces. This is done with a scoring tool that can be easily made by grinding the hard end (not the tang end) of a three-corner file to a sharp point — I have used various other things already made, such as an ice pick and a carbide scriber.

This scoring is done by scribing along a steel straightedge held diagonally from corner to corner of the lap. Make scribes as deeply as possible, using only one pass; space them ⅜ inches apart over the entire surface. Then do the same in the opposite direction, which will give a diamond-shape grid effect.

The reason for one pass only is that a second pass will not likely follow the first in angle and therefore produce too wide a groove.

All this will come full-blown if one purchases the laps from toolmaker suppliers. I suppose the theory in scoring is that the grooves provide a residual area for the abrasive to collect. All this scratching of lines will raise small burrs upon the surface which should be removed by rubbing the plate on fine emery paper.

One more very important implement before honing. You should have a small triangle of wood with a series of inked lines at whatever angle to the bottom of the triangle is desired for the cutting edge being honed. I use 32 degree for both plane irons and general-purpose chisels.

The triangle is put bottom down on the lapping plate next to the iron that is going to be honed. Then the honing guide is adjusted until the back of the iron coincides with the lines on the triangle.

Marked block for setting the blade in the honing guide —

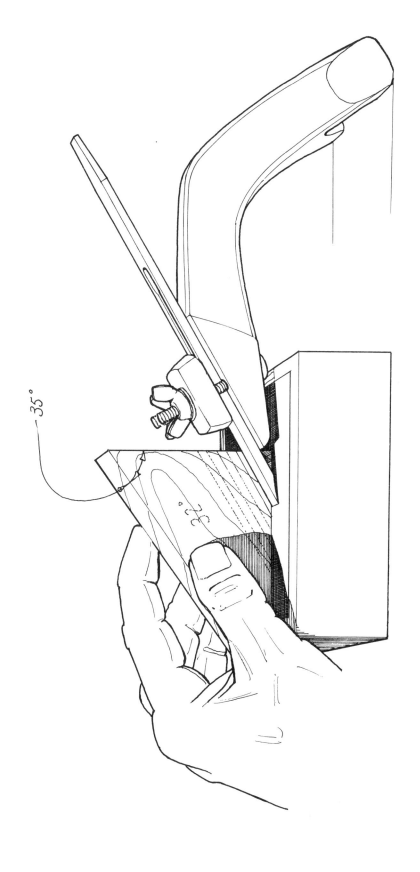

35°

Marked block laid on the stone alongside the blade establishes the angle wanted for honing the beveled edge.

Adjustment is made by sliding the blade in or out of the honing guide.

With the last word of the previous paragraph, I took a leave of writing, "a busman's holiday" as we say, to further explore this revolutionary business of sharpening with diamond – revolutionary, that is, to the everyday workman. This holiday led me in many directions, some marginally within the scope of this book.

First, I sharpened with diamond the hundreds of edges which reside here, and I mean hundreds: plane irons, chisels of all sizes and descriptions, carving gouges, both incanal and paring, hatchets and axes, drawknives, adzes, and even the kitchen knives. Oh, yes, and the turned-edge scrapers, but more about the scrapers in another section.

A phone call to the manufacturer of the diamond compound was rewarding. Even though I had tried all materials such as cast iron, glass, copper, brass, steel and hardwood, only the cast iron seemed to work well. What was his recommendation for a honing plate? He confirmed my finding of cast iron as the only suitable material. Was anyone using this compound to produce sharp edges? Yes, he knew of some disposable-blade makers, but they guarded their methods closely.

In terms of grit, what did one micron measure out? 14,000! Infinite when it is compared to the finest common abrasive at 600 grit.

While on the subject of micron, let's put it in the language that those of us who went to the little red schoolhouse can readily understand.

A micron is one thousandth of a millimeter. Most of our everyday accurate rules divide the inch into 32nds. Now the millimeter and the 32nd are, for our purposes, the same size (.039+ for the former and .032+ for the latter). So the micron divides our 32nd of an inch into one thousand pieces!

When I went to my barber the diamond lapping plate went with me and I left it with him, suggesting that he try it out. He was, when later I called, ecstatic about it — he just had to have one. If anyone in our society knows about sharp edges, it is a barber.

At my woodworking society, I cornered a surgeon who works wood as a hobby and I said, "How do you sharpen your scalpels?"

"Oh! We don't do that – we buy disposables."

"Do you maybe have one of the sharpenable kind?"

"No," he replied with a chuckle, "I am not that old! But I will tell you what happened to us in Korea. There were no disposables and none of us could sharpen what we had. Know what we did? We took our scalpels to the barbers for them to sharpen them for us!"

While this holiday was going on a circumstance happened that causes me to write about the strike button on a plane. I had previously thought but dismissed the idea of writing about the strike button because it involved physics, a science about which I know very little.

The word itself makes me shudder because my mother used it in a different context. As a boy, whenever I would feel the flu or other disorder coming on, I would attempt to hide it. But mother, in the manner of mothers everywhere, would inevitably discover it quickly.

"You look pale to me, I believe you should have some physic." To which father would chime in, "Yes, he should have a good dose of salts." That being epsom salts in a glass of water! It was the worst possible sentence; better to be sick.

Back to the circumstance, it goes like this. A committee member from one of my woodworking societies phoned me to say that the board of directors had decided to reward the outgoing president with a present. Would I take the $25.00 that was available, and search the market for a suitable plane or other tool for the occasion?

I met the assignment by taking one of my new planes and presenting it, in a few days, to the caller. He operates a sharpening service for power tools. He loved it! Fondled and caressed it, saying how beautiful the wood and workmanship was. I love such talk and cannot get enough of it.

All the while he keeps fondling the brass strike button.

"You know what that button does?" I asked.

"No," he replied.

"When you strike it with a hammer, that causes the iron to recede."

"Oh, that goes all the way through to the cutter?"

"No, you see, it is a matter of physics."

I explained that when the button is struck with a hammer, the plane tends to go forward, but the mass of the iron, not being integral with the wood, tends to hold its original position.

"Are you going to put that in your book?"

"No!"

"I think that you should," he insisted. So here it is, for the better or worse.

I hope that no one well versed in physics reads it.

While on this R. & D. holiday, there was another problem that needed solution. I needed to find a suitable flotant. Light oil is the normal medium for this but it is so messy that it was ruled out. This flotant must be cheap, readily available, and non-rusting.

I was already using a soluble-in-water emulsion used primarily by the grinding industry and it was excellent for the job, but not readily available universally.

Experiments with various liquid-soap combinations were not the answer. I even stepped back in time and tried spittle which was excellent too! But for obvious reasons, it was ruled out also.

Then the answer came, after a too-long period of gestation for such a simple solution. Ethylene glycol, the stuff that is in your auto radiator. It met all the necessary criteria.

Holiday is over. Your wordsmith is now back with the pen and all necessary information to finish this section. There is no reason to change or modify that which has been written before this break, except perhaps in the area of the diamond hone.

I have found that the ones with the solid diamond surface are more versatile. For instance, a small edge such as ¼-inch or smaller chisel, when rubbed along the interrupted surface (as in the previous recommendation of the diamond stone) tend to "stub their toe" on the holes. I use the solid diamond hones now to the exclusion of all others.

Although my inventory of diamond compound consists of several grades, I recommend that you start out with only one grade. The #1 strong can be your workhorse; any others can come later as deemed to be necessary.

Now that we have all of the accouterments necessary, let's you and I hone either a chisel or plane iron, working together much as we did previously when we built the plane together.

First, let us assume that we have a hollowed bevel produced by any method at all — the grinder and guide which I have described, or hand guided at the bench grinder, or hollowed out with a scythe stone.

This latter is not said in levity, for I know a man who does just this by using a scythe stone, rounded out with another scythe stone then applied to the bevel with a wood guide to keep it within bounds.

To repeat, we put the tool in the holder part of the honing guide and tighten loosely. Now we put this assembly on the honing station with the tool edge resting on the stationary diamond surface of whatever you have chosen to be the diamond medium for the first, or coarse, honing.

Next, with the little triangular wood gauge, adjust the tool in its holder to coincide with any one of the marks; then tighten the thumb nuts securely.

Now dip the edge in the flotant and proceed to hone the edge back and forth. Inspect it frequently until the edge shows a new edge across — do not overdo it, for this new edge will happen quickly.

Remember, I am doing it too. The black color showing in the flotant is composed of steel particles, alerting me that things are happening fast.

With a piece of hardwood, run across the new edge, wipe away the burr which has formed.

The first phase of honing is completed, and we go to the cast-iron lapping plate placed directly behind the stationary one we have just used.

If it has not already been done, put a judicious amount (6 or 8 dabs about the size of a common pin head) of the #1 strong compound at various locations and rub with a fingertip to coat the surface rather completely.

Now, again dipping the edge in the flotant, proceed to hone as before. This will be a much slower job.

After a few minutes of this, I find upon inspection, my narrow honed edge appears to have a mirror polish. I again wipe off the wire or burr edge.

Now, move the hone to the edge and hone the flat back of the iron until the mirror shows here and all the way across.

All these operations are accomplished without removing the tool from

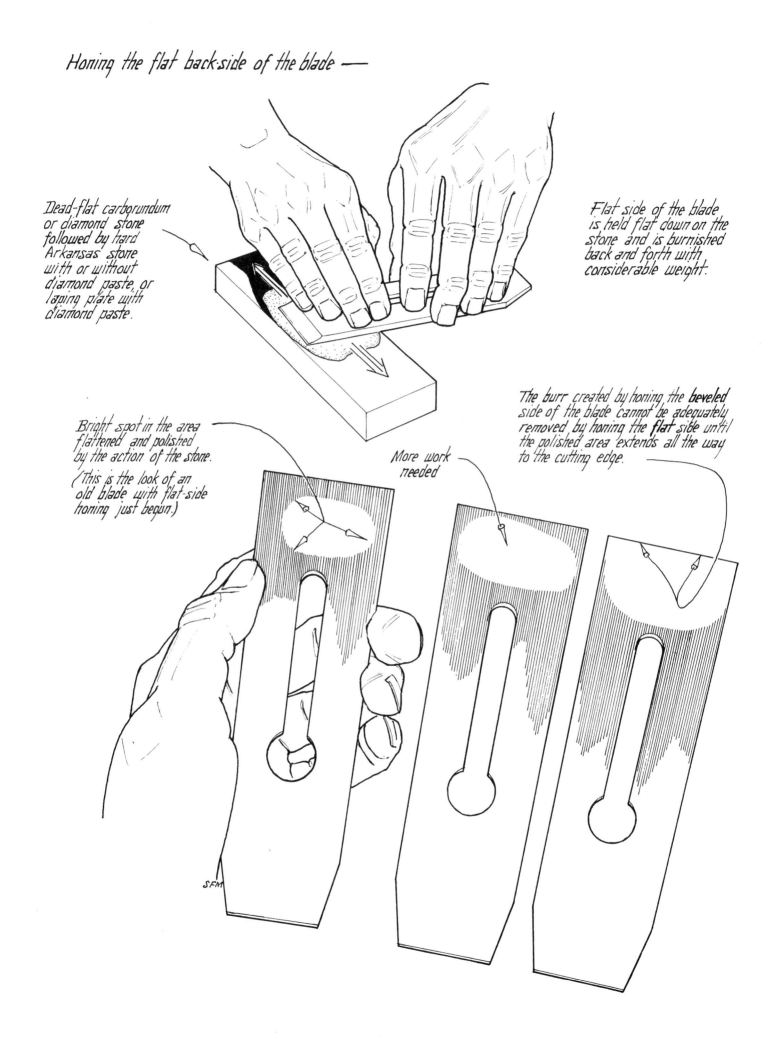

Honing the flat back-side of the blade —

Dead-flat carborundum or diamond stone followed by hard Arkansas stone with or without diamond paste, or laping plate with diamond paste.

Flat side of the blade is held flat down on the stone and is burnished back and forth with considerable weight.

Bright spot in the area flattened and polished by the action of the stone.

(This is the look of an old blade with flat-side honing just begun.)

More work needed

The burr created by honing the **beveled** side of the blade cannot be adequately removed by honing the **flat** side until the polished area extends all the way to the cutting edge.

S.F.M.

the holder.

When you test the edge and it meets your test for sharpness, the job is finished and the tool may be removed from the holder. But first, you may want to scribe a scratch across the tool, using the top of the holder bar for a guide. This will allow putting it back in the holder at the same angle next time.

Mine took less than 5 minutes but I suspect that yours took somewhat longer. But each time will take a shorter period, because all the edges will be in better shape to start with.

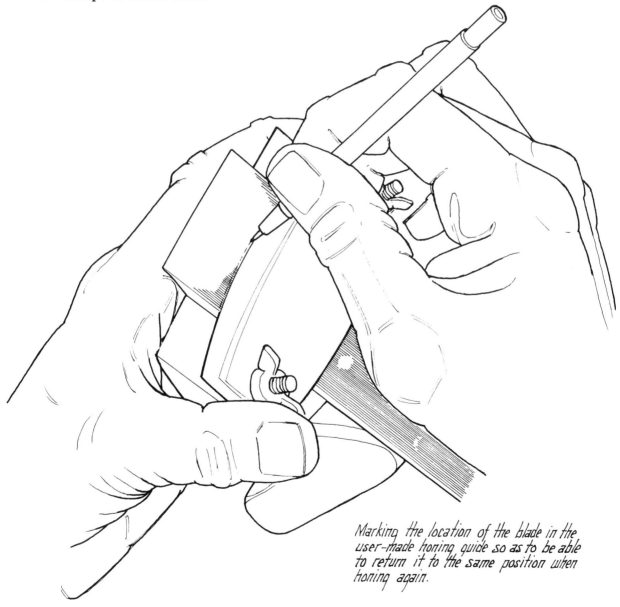

Marking the location of the blade in the user-made honing guide so as to be able to return it to the same position when honing again.

The Turned-Edge Scraper

The turned-edge scraper is the proper adjunct to the plane. As such, it properly belongs in this book.

What is the history of it? Who knows? My search for its origin has been unrewarding.

The previously mentioned Joseph Moxon is glaringly silent on the subject. But Edward Knight in his voluminous *American Mechanical Dictionary* (1877) comes full-blown on the subject. Sometime between the late 1600s and the mid-1800s, the turned-edge scraper must have evolved.

Though actually primitive in its conception, this tool would have to be of momentous importance to craftsmen in wood right up to and including to-morrow.

It was a nice day in early June. The poet said, "Then if ever come perfect days" – auspicious words.

A pretty little Alden-designed schooner was tied up to a floating dock. Her winter cover of canvas was already removed. Her skipper was aboard; maybe he was living aboard. Anyway, he was supervising her recommissioning. It was during those more or less placid years between the two world wars, when top-rate craftsmen such as I am about to describe were paid fifty cents per hour for their nine-hour days and six-day weeks.

Three men came down the runway at a little before seven o'clock — there was no whistle, everyone knew that the day started at seven. A whistle would be silly and superfluous.

The man in the lead was an old man. He had a wooden box under his arm. In it and in his overalls pockets were all the necessary tools to do his allotted job, which was to refinish the rail caps. They are the mahogany top of the bulwarks that went completely around the vessel.

The second man was a young, slightly built man, carrying a bucket in which he also had the tools that he needed, which were turned-edge scrapers.

The third man, a very young man, was carrying a forty-pound steel tool box. He was a machinist, as marine mechanics were called in those days. He was going to work on the little four-cylinder Red Wing engine in back of the cabin companionway stairs. Red Wings were derisively said to have blue clay cylinders and gutta percha valves.

The skipper greeted the old man warmly at the rail, for he knew him well and knew that he could do it all, having spent a lifetime at it.

To the next man with the bucket he offered a terse, "I'll tend you at the halyards," for he was going aloft in a bosun's chair to scrape both Douglas fir masts and refinish them.

The third and last over the rail was greeted with a cold stare as the skipper reached for the heavy tool box, not to make it any easier but to ensure that the sharp corners did not touch any varnish work and thereby produce a scratch.

"Don't step anywhere but on those boards," he ordered.

A track of loose scrap boards had been laid across the deck from the rail to the cabin companionway.

They were there because all "machinists" were, rightly or wrongly, accused of having grease and oil on the soles of their shoes – anathema to holy-stoned decks.

Such were the days when the wooden plane and turned-edge scraper held sway.

These men need not go unnamed.

The old man was Cushman ("Cush") Gray. He could do it all, having built boats, and he was as much at home upstairs in the jointer shop as in the planking crew. I recently restored, for its owner, a lignum vitae jack plane which Cush had made so many years ago. Cush had even had a stint of skippering.

The name of the young man in the bosun's chair eludes my memory. But the machinist's name does not, for it was this writer before turning from the machinist lathe and socket wrenches to working of wood fibers.

Cush, like his counterparts in the yacht yards and cabinet shops worldwide, was a master of the turned-edge scraper. It is a tool that produces such a surface on wood that "one can seem to look into the very wood itself," a vast improvement on the finely scratched surface produced by abrasive paper.

Cush, again like some of his counterparts, spent no money for his scraper tooling. All he needed was a few three-inch pieces cut from a cast-off hand saw, and two pieces of cast-off three-sided files with their ends broken off to shorten them up to better fit in overall pockets.

One of the files would be used to sharpen a new bevel on the blade and the other one, ground, honed, and polished by hand to a "slippery" surface, would be the burnisher with which to turn the edge.

The blade and the burnisher could then, as now, be purchased at the hardware stores. But they would not be superior for the job at hand. Because the blade then, as now, was and is made from "saw plate" steel and the burnisher of file hard steel then and now.

Cush brought out the original beauty of those mahogany rails, and it could not have been done with any other tool than with the turned-edge scraper.

Before we go further, let's examine this action that, in the English language, we term "scraping."

It is ancient! As soon as man discovered the art of chipping flinty stone to a sharp edge, he used those sharp edges to scrape into shape his useful items of wood, shell and bone.

It has been said that no culture has ever been discovered in this world that did not have these common denominators: a language, a religion, and a music. To this I would add, "They were all scrapers"; even today there is no other way.

Our abrasive paper and grinding wheels of today are but the workings of technology upon the aboriginal's flinty materials. "Abrade" and "Cleave" are the two terms used to denote the two methods that we use to smooth or "clean up" wood as it relates to the cabinetmaker.

My unabridged dictionary says of Abrade, "to waste by friction"; of the word Cleave, "to divide by force." The axe Cleaves, the plane Cleaves and the turned-edge scraper Cleaves. The latter two are the only precision hand tools to do so.

The turned-edge scraper, made from the quite soft and fileable steel which is used to make hand saws, needs no explanation. This simple and obtainable tool has one great drawback. It is so soft that its turned edge is short-lived.

I needed a better material for the tool, a material whose edge-life could be measured in hours rather than minutes. I set myself upon this task.

My first candidate was spring steel. With hacksaw in hand, I started cutting up old automobile springs.

Cut up spring leaves with a hand hacksaw, you ask?

Yes, and it can be done rather easily, as this story and the learned lesson explains.

I started my professional life back in the late 1920s as an automobile mechanic. The old cars and poor roads of those years were cause for much spring breakage in the period cars. A large percentage of our work was repairing springs. To do this, we cannibalized leaves from discarded springs.

These were never the proper length for the job at hand. So, being unable to cut them to fit, we would take them to the blacksmith shop, where the smith would heat them to red heat in the forge and, with a hot cutter used on the anvil, would quickly sever the leaf at the proper length; a rather time-consuming process, especially as the blacksmith was not always readily available.

One day an itinerant salesman appeared on the shop floor and announced that he had for sale hacksaw blades that were capable of sawing spring leaves. He called for one on which to demonstrate and one was quickly produced from the scrap pile and put in a vise for him.

Sure enough, in five minutes or so he had accomplished what might take an hour or even two to get done at the blacksmith.

The blades were expensive but fabulous in what they could accomplish. We all bought a few.

He disappeared through the door, never to be seen again. He knew that it would not be long before we would discover that his blades were no better than the ones we already had. His technique of heavy downward pressure and slow forward speed worked with any blade.

What he had sold us was a technique. It was well worth the price and has served me well many times.

To get back to the business at hand. The steel from automobile spring leaves was little if any better than the hand saw material. If the truth be known, they are probably one and the same steel.

Those who know and appreciate fine hand saws will remember the Disston saws with the words "London Spring" engraved upon them. The meaning was that they were made of English spring steel. These were among the best saws that were ever produced by anyone.

Still questing, I remembered that some of the "irons" made for the Stanley type metal planes were fileable if one used my learned technique of excessive pressure and slow speed. These filed "irons" were a distinct improvement over the conventional saw plate material, doubling the life expectancy of that fragile turned edge.

Success begets success. Perhaps some harder material yet may be turned – cast steel plane irons perhaps. But what to use for a burnisher?

The plane iron would be as hard as the commercial burnisher, therefore not likely to perform well, if at all. Tungsten carbide, that hardest of the common materials which we have to work with, might do as a burnisher. But where to get a round shaft of the stuff?

Some bedroom pondering brought back the memory that in the tool storage were some solid carbide router bits. They proved to be three inches long with only one inch of one end worked into a cutter. This cutter end, imbedded in a wood handle, left two inches of smooth-ground one-quarter-inch diameter stock which became a perfect burnisher after diamond honing it to a gleaming finish.

Now to turn the edge on some really hard material: "cast steel." Groundbreaking this would be — to the best of my knowledge.

An old Charles Buck plane iron of this material was prepared in this manner.

First, it was hollow ground to an acute angle of 22 degrees; after which it was carefully diamond sharpened and finally honed with number one diamond compound to the ultimate sharp edge which this material is capable of, indeed, famous for.

With the modified plane blade held in a vise, the edge upward, and a well lubricated and polished carbide burnisher in hand, I proceeded, ever so carefully, to do the impossible: to turn or bend that edge over.

After a few passes, even my age-impaired hearing could hear a crinkling sound. The edge was fracturing, not bending or turning.

Several tries later, I was to learn the technique of coaxing the edge over. Mostly it was a matter of pressure, about as much as one uses to spread butter on a slice of bread.

Now I regularly turn edges whose working life is at least ten times that of their cousins of saw steel.

Edges sharpened and honed to all angles up to the classic square, or ninety degree, can also be turned on hard material. More pressure is needed to turn the blunter angles.

Don't forget to ease off those two corners of the edge a few thousandths, they are troublemakers.

I make and epoxy onto the end of all of my flat scrapers a "D" handle (clearly shown in the photos) of any available hardwood. There are two important reasons for this.

Number one, the art of turning the edge is not an exact one in terms of the angle produced. So this handle allows for automatic adjustment to the optimum best cutting angle, from vertical to near parallel with the work.

Number two, it is completely comfortable for long or short stints of scraping.

I close this section with this observation: from the flat top of the mahogany or walnut table to the intricate curves of the integral handle of a coco bolo plane, the smooth plane, gouge, skew chisel and turned-edge scraper will do it better than abrasive paper, and with vastly more satisfaction to the craftsman.

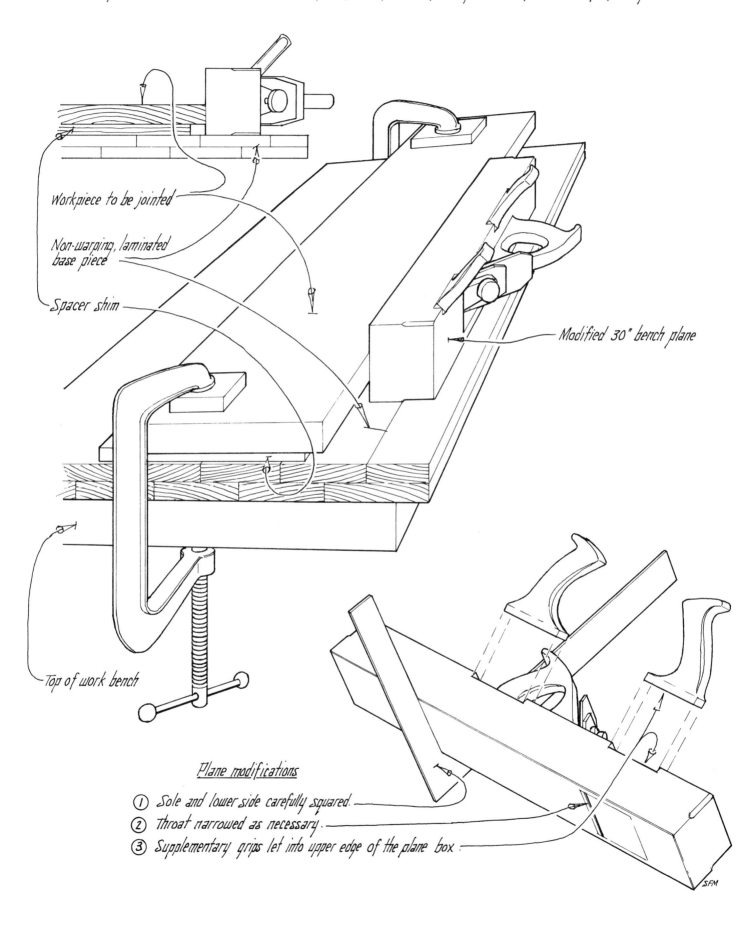

Chuting board —— To insure cutting of a right-angled edge when jointing boards or plank for edge-glueing ——

Workpiece to be jointed

Non-warping, laminated base piece

Spacer shim

Modified 30" bench plane

Top of work bench

Plane modifications

① Sole and lower side carefully squared.
② Throat narrowed as necessary.
③ Supplementary grips let into upper edge of the plane box.

S.F.M.

The Chute Board

All my long life the jointing up of boards for table tops, or for whatever, has been time-consuming and anything but satisfying after the job was completed; knowing as I did, that even if the joint was satisfactory, too much had depended upon good fortune and extreme pressures with the long bar clamps.

I even built a long jointer plane with a permanent guide or fence at a right angle to the bottom — all to no avail. I could not maintain a square edge for the whole length of the board.

My consideration of the problem led me to the chute board.

Now the chute board is not a new idea; it has been around for a century at least. This tooling involved a very special plane and a cast-iron "box" in which the plane was very closely guided when in use. Its principal function was to true up ill-fitting miter joints. The plane and its use were of no help to my problem.

After weeks of thinking, a plan began to unfold in my mind.

It was plain that a plank or base was needed to build a device upon. To make this work-holder as adaptable as possible, it was first necessary to determine what its length should be. It could be of any length, but storage room and area to use it in dictated that it be six feet long by twelve inches wide, in my case. So I set about edge-glueing hardwood boards until there were two boards, six feet long by 12" wide.

These were carefully surfaced in a planer, making them ¾ inch thick, after which they were glued together, making a base 1½" thick. All this laminating was done to ensure as best as possible that it would not, in time, warp and as a result have a twist, or be out of wind.

How this was later built upon can best be determined by referring to the drawing.

The holder completed, now a plane was needed.

Would I build a new one?

No! There are too many abandoned thirty-inch wooden planes around.

Having three myself, I selected one for rebuilding. Any one of them was an excellent candidate for the job because the wood had become so stabilized from age that it could be expected to stay as flat on the sole as the reworking of it would produce.

First, of course, the throat was badly worn. A carefully let-in adjustable rosewood piece, two inches long by ⅜" thick, took care of this nicely.

Next, the side of the plane, upon which it would run, was carefully worked square with the sole. Of course, my dislike for the wedge system of holding the iron (remember earlier my being very emphatic about that?) caused me to install the toggle for that purpose.

Unlike most things "cooked up" from "whole cloth," this was a complete success from the first trial, delivering perfect joints without the scalloping produced by power jointers.

Later I was to add two handles to the plane, set at 45 degrees to the bottom/side. Also a squirt or two of the new silicone lubricant gives the plane a feeling that it is gliding on ball bearings.

Au revoir.